RUNNING ADVENTURES SCOTLAND

RUNNING ADVENTURES SCOTLAND

25 INSPIRATIONAL RUNS IN SCOTLAND'S WILD PLACES

ROSS BRANNIGAN

Vertebrate Publishing, Sheffield
www.adventurebooks.com

RUNNING ADVENTURES SCOTLAND

25 INSPIRATIONAL RUNS IN SCOTLAND'S WILD PLACES

ROSS BRANNIGAN

 First published in 2022 by Vertebrate Publishing.

Vertebrate Publishing, Omega Court, 352 Cemetery Road, Sheffield S11 8FT, United Kingdom.
www.adventurebooks.com

Copyright © 2022 Ross Brannigan and Vertebrate Publishing Ltd.

Ross Brannigan has asserted his rights under the Copyright, Designs and Patents Act 1988 to be identified as author of this work.

A CIP catalogue record for this book is available from the British Library.

ISBN 978-1-83981-068-8 (Paperback)
ISBN 978-1-83981-166-1 (Ebook)

All rights reserved. No part of this work covered by the copyright herein may be reproduced or used in any form or by any means – graphic, electronic, or mechanised, including photocopying, recording, taping, or information storage and retrieval systems – without the written permission of the publisher.

Front cover *Dougie Harvey on Cir Mhòr, Arran, in morning light above a cloud inversion after a high bivvy* (route 22). © Finlay Wild.

Back cover (L–R) *River crossing in Glen Coe* (route 05), *Bothy on Loch Lomond* (route 25), *Skirting Sgùrr Beag looking west to Creag nan Damh* (route 08), *Looking over Loch Tay from Meall Greigh* (route 18), *On the West Highland Way near Tyndrum* (route 25), *Views across the Trossachs* (route 15).

Opposite page *Snow slope* (route 14).

Photography by **Ross Brannigan** unless otherwise credited.

Mapping contains data from OS © Crown copyright and database right (2022) and © OpenStreetMap contributors, **Openstreetmap.org/copyright**

Relief shading produced from data derived from U.S. Geological Survey, National Geospatial Program.

Cartography by Richard Ross, Active Maps Ltd. – www.activemaps.co.uk

Edited by Helen Parry, cover design by Jane Beagley, internal layout and production by Rosie Edwards.
www.adventurebooks.com

Printed and bound in Europe by Latitude Press.

Vertebrate Publishing is committed to printing on paper from sustainable sources.

Every effort has been made to achieve accuracy of the information in this guidebook. The authors, publishers and copyright owners can take no responsibility for: loss or injury (including fatal) to persons; loss or damage to property or equipment; trespass, irresponsible behaviour or any other mishap that may be suffered as a result of following the route descriptions or advice offered in this guidebook. The inclusion of a track or path as part of a route, or otherwise recommended, in this guidebook does not guarantee that the track or path will remain a right of way. If conflict with landowners arises we advise that you act politely and leave by the shortest route available. If the matter needs to be taken further then please take it up with the relevant authority.

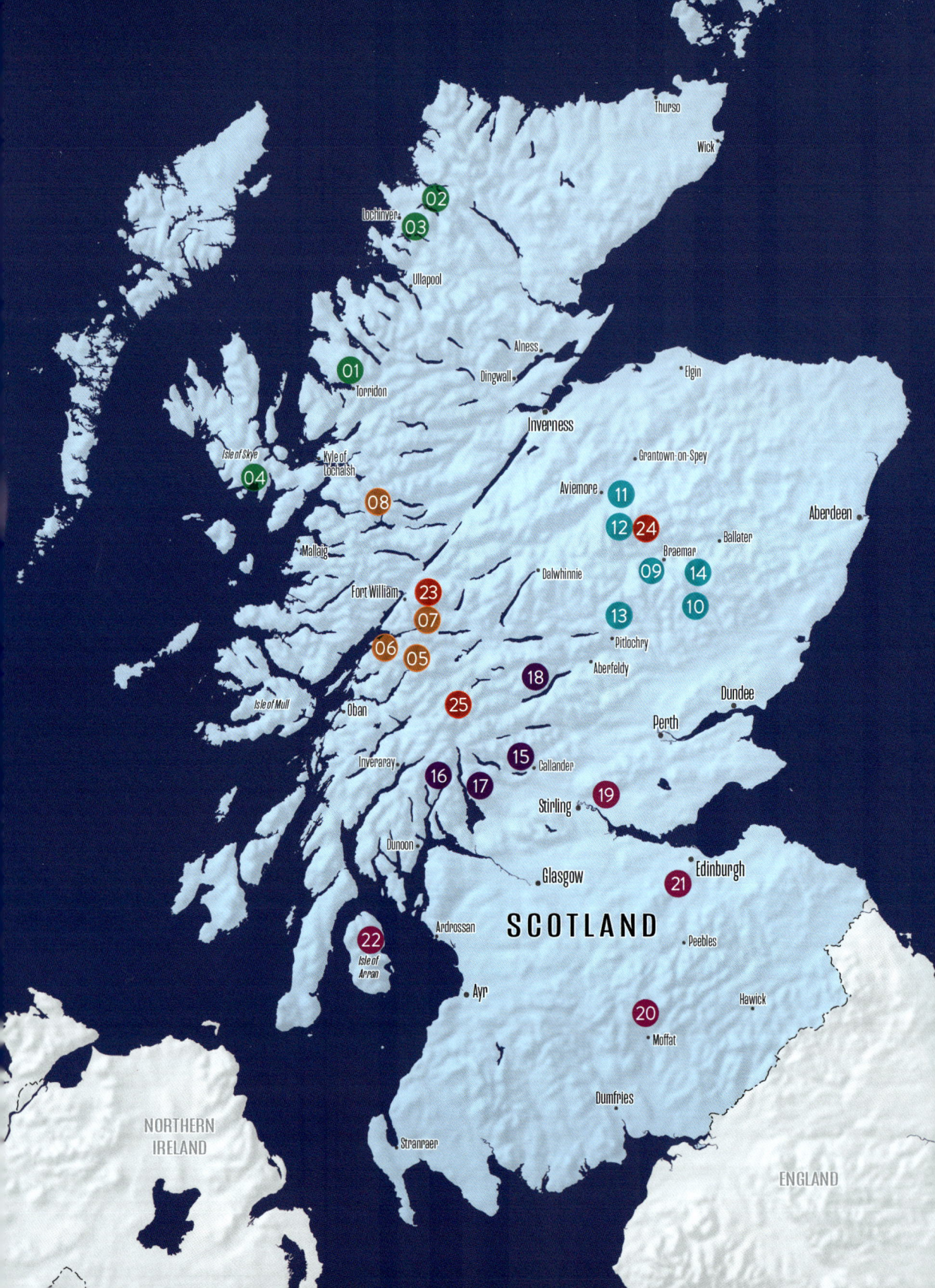

CONTENTS

INTRODUCTION IX
ACKNOWLEDGEMENTS IX
HOW TO USE THIS BOOK IX
FITNESS X
ENVIRONMENT AND SUSTAINABILITY XI
CAMPING AND CAMPERVANS XII
SAFETY XIII
HISTORY, NAMES AND LANGUAGE XV

NORTH WEST HIGHLANDS
01 Beinn Alligin *10km* 03
02 Quinag – three Corbetts *14km* 09
03 Suilven *20km* 15
04 Sgùrr na Strì and Camasunary *23km* 21

WESTERN HIGHLANDS
05 Glen Coe's Two Lairigs *14km* 29
06 Beinn a' Bheithir – the Ballachulish Horseshoe *16km* . . . 35
07 Ring of Steall *17km* 41
08 South Glen Shiel Ridge – seven Munros in a day *27km* . . . 47

CAIRNGORMS
09 Morrone *11km* 55
10 Mayar, Driesh and Corrie Fee *15km* 61
11 Meall a' Bhuachaille *16km* 67
12 Cairngorm Plateau *20km* 73
13 Beinn a' Ghlo *22km* 79
14 White Mounth circuit *29km* 85

SOUTHERN HIGHLANDS
15 Ben Ledi *11km* 93
16 The Cobbler – Ben Arthur *11km* 99
17 Ben Lomond via the Ptarmigan Ridge *12km* 105
18 Ben Lawers *22km* 111

CENTRAL & SOUTHERN SCOTLAND
19 Heart of the Ochils *12km* 119
20 Hart Fell Horseshoe *17km* 125
21 Pentland Skyline *23km* 131
22 Glen Rosa Horseshoe, Isle of Arran *26km* 137

MULTI-DAY ROUTES
23 Tranter's Round *63km* 145
24 Five bothies in the Cairngorms *64km* 153
25 West Highland Way – Scotland's classic trail *153km* . . . 161

MORE LIKE THIS 171
CONTACTS 174

Download the Running Adventures Scotland GPX files from www.adventurebooks.com/RAS-GPX

INTRODUCTION

Scotland: the land of myths and legends, mountains and glens, lochs and rivers. It is home to some of the last remaining wilderness in the UK, with dramatic landscapes and fascinating wildlife.

This book is your running guide to Scotland's wild places. Each route will take you on an adventure; whether that is over a mountain (or several), through remote glens, or as part of a longer journey – each of them will stay with you.

You will learn more about what makes Scotland such an incredible place to visit, find out about local history and culture, and see some beautiful places.

Scotland has a long history of hill running. Once used by kings as a test of fitness, the sport of hill running has evolved over the years and is now comprised of a close community of like-minded folks who love nothing more than a boggy day out on these incredible hills.

Each route has been carefully selected. One might be host to a classic Scottish hill race; another could be part of a 'round' or 'fastest known time' route; another may have a cultural significance; and many are simply absolute bangers that are adored by runners across Scotland. In fact, they are so loved that you will find quotes from some of these runners at the start of each route.

I have picked out what I feel are the iconic routes you just *have* to run. There are sublime ridges, amazing trails and, in every direction, sensational views (when they aren't obscured by cloud, of course).

What I hope you find as you follow this guide is that Scotland is a beautiful place. However, it is under threat. The climate and biodiversity crises are taking their toll on this landscape, as are the increasing visitor numbers.

So, wherever you go, make sure to leave no trace, keep to paths as much as you can and consider giving back to help protect and enhance this amazing landscape for future generations.

ACKNOWLEDGEMENTS

There are a few people I would like to acknowledge in the writing of this book. First and foremost, despite the times my brother and I moaned our way up yet another sodden Munro on yet another caravan trip to the deepest depths of Scotland, I have to thank my parents. Without them, I would not have grown up with the passion for the hills and the country that I have now, and so this book would not have existed. In the same vein, I have to thank the rest of my family, who you will more than likely come across if you go into the Ochil Hills. They have been nothing but encouraging. In particular, Gran and Pops, who have spent many, many hours sat at the kitchen table over tea and baking, listening to my tall tales, and who have always pushed me to take every opportunity and have read every piece of writing I produce.

Thanks as well to the friends who have come out on adventures with me, regularly to bleak places in miserable weather, but also many stunning days. Thanks to you all – you know who you are. Particular mention needs to go to Finlay Wild, who provided the exceptional cover artwork for the book, and to all the incredible runners who provided quotes for each of the routes.

Thank you to the team at Vertebrate Publishing, particularly Kirsty Reade who gave me a commission that I could only dream of having.

Finally, a massive thank you to my partner, Bo. Without complaint, she followed me across the country, exploring the mountains, being a model for most of the photography, listening to my doubts and fears, and for convincing me that a day is never complete without a *lekker kopje koffie en cake*. Thank you.

HOW TO USE THIS BOOK

In each of the routes, you will find a quick overview of the main statistics (distance, ascent, time), along with some insights on the terrain. Each route is graded out of five for difficulty (with 1/5 denoting a straightforward route and 5/5 indicating a

OPPOSITE *EARLY STAGES OF SOUTH GLEN SHIEL RIDGE* (ROUTE 08)

MAOL CHINN-DEARG LOOKING TOWARDS AONACH AIR CHRITH (ROUTE 08)

technical route) and for the amount of bogs you may encounter (with 1/5 meaning you may still have dry feet at the end of the route but if it's a 5/5 there is no chance your feet will stay dry). I will tell you a bit about why this route is 'ace', 'superb' or 'cracking', before providing step-by-step directions for the route. There is also loads of useful information on public transport, parking, ways to shorten or extend the route and details of the best cafes and pubs to enjoy after your run.

NAVIGATION

Directions are provided for each route, along with a map of the route to give you a good sense of orientation. GPX files for the routes can be downloaded (see page VII); they can then be uploaded on to a GPS device to aid navigation.

GPS devices are a great navigational aid, but you should always carry a paper map and compass, and know how to use them. I have recommended a map for each route. There are some great apps to use on your phone, including OS Locate from Ordnance Survey, which are helpful to position yourself, but be aware that phone batteries can perish quickly in the cold, and you might find that you have no signal in many remote areas of Scotland.

While every effort has been made to ensure accuracy within the directions and descriptions in this book, things change and we are unable to guarantee that every detail will be correct. For this reason, the routes in this book are guides only and must be planned and run with care. Treat the stated distance and ascent as guidelines and exercise caution if part of a GPX file or some information in the text appears at odds with the route on the ground. A comparison between the GPX file and map should see you on the right track.

TRANSPORT

Where possible, I have included public transport links for the routes. Bus and train timetables are available at **www.travelinescotland.com** Details about car parking are also provided.

FITNESS

I won't beat about the bush: you will be going up hills. And down them.

I have kept the routes as varied as possible, with some shorter days and some epic routes, helping you have fun and find something at your level. Nevertheless, be prepared to go up and down some big lumps and, occasionally, over some rough ground.

Where I say 'rough', think rocks hidden under thick grass and lots of heather. Where I say 'technical' this often refers to rocky, sometimes exposed places, such as narrow ridges.

I would suggest you have experience of walking in the hills before taking on some of the more

technical routes in this book. Trail running isn't immediately transferable to hill running either, so do make sure you've got some experience of being in the hills before heading out.

ENVIRONMENT AND SUSTAINABILITY

As you follow the routes in this book through the awe-inspiring landscape that is Scotland, it is important to be mindful of your behaviour and the environment around you so that people can continue to enjoy these places in the future.

As hill runners, the lure of a bog, bouncy castle of heather or scree slope is often difficult to resist. While in many cases you should certainly go out and enjoy yourself, keep an eye out for any signs that it might not be a great idea. Here are some pointers to help you enjoy running in Scotland responsibly.

Stick to paths and trods where possible

There are a few reasons for this. Firstly, erosion in areas of high visitor numbers can see multiple scars appear on the hillside instead of a single track. Not only is this ugly to look at, but it also causes soil degradation and can cause rocks and soil to wash away in heavy rain, adding to the problem. Peat is one of the biggest carbon capture systems on the planet, so protecting it is vitally important to the environment.

Secondly, small flora suffer from being repeatedly stomped on, so help our little alpine plants by sticking to the path.

Thirdly, particularly in spring and summer, watch out for ground-nesting birds. These are birds who – as the name suggests – lay their eggs in the tall grasses and heath of the hillsides. It can be difficult to spot a nest, but there are a few signs to watch out for:

- adult birds feigning injury to draw you away from the nest (notable for grouse or ptarmigan);
- loud alarm calls or even dive-bombing;
- birds circling above you to draw you away.

Lastly, scree is excellent fun, but many scree slopes are home to birds or fragile plants. A lot of the popular scree slopes are run-out now, but it is better to stick to the used ones rather than fresh ones as the latter could be home to a number of plants and animals.

Follow the Scottish Outdoor Access Code

We will look in detail at the Scottish Outdoor Access Code overleaf, but the key things to bear in mind here are:

- leave no trace;
- respect the environment.

Leaving no trace simply means leaving no sign of your being there. Take your litter home or put it in a bin. If you are camping, do not light fires or move stones around that are in the ground, and make sure you only stay a night or two. If you need to 'go', dig a little hole in the ground, cover it up and put your loo roll in a bin (this might require using a sandwich bag). Wet wipes (or baby wipes) do not decompose, so we will all be reminded of your business for the rest of time – take them home.

Respecting the environment means following the advice above about paths, avoiding disturbance of plants and animals and protecting geological features. You are visiting these areas because of their natural beauty, so make sure you leave them the way you found them.

If you run with a dog, keep them under control around farm animals and breeding birds. Farmers have the right to shoot a dog if they feel it is worrying their livestock.

Consider giving back to the places you visit
Throughout this book, I draw your attention to various groups and charities who care for the areas you are visiting. If you enjoyed visiting, do consider making a donation to the charity mentioned in association with the route, or perhaps returning to carry out voluntary work.

Scotland's environment is not immune to the impact of the climate emergency, ecological imbalances and issues caused by visitors. Anything we can do to help protect these landscapes is vital to ensuring more people can experience wild places, while helping to conserve and restore them.

SCOTTISH OUTDOOR ACCESS CODE
You are in luck! Scotland has some of the best access rights in the entire world. The only condition is that you don't behave like an eejit, as we say. In general, you are free to go where you wish in Scotland and camp where you like, so long as you use common sense and act responsibly.

There are three basic rules forming the Scottish Outdoor Access Code:

- Take responsibility for your own actions.
- Respect the interests of others.
- Care for the environment.

Be mindful of shooting activities on the hills and moors. Read more at **www.outdooraccess-scotland.scot**

CAMPING AND CAMPERVANS
CAMPING
The responsibilities and sustainability aspects of wild camping are covered within the Scottish Outdoor Access Code; more information is available at **www.outdooraccess-scotland.scot**

CAMPERVANS
For more and more people, a campervan is the go-to accommodation for outdoor trips – they are becoming an increasingly frequent sight on Scotland's roads. There are a few things to remember as you take your campervan around Scotland:

- Leave no trace of your being there.
- Arrive late, leave early.
- You are allowed to park in lay-bys (small bays next to a road), but technically not allowed to stay overnight in car parks without permission from the landowner.
- Do *not* camp in passing places – these are spaces on single-track roads that people use to pass cars coming in the opposite direction. They will often have a sign designating it as a passing place. Parking in these is very much frowned upon, especially in the Highlands where they are essential for locals to get around.
- Do not block gates or access points – you could stop locals or farmers getting around or, at worst, prevent access for emergency service vehicles.
- Be prepared to do some reversing on single-track roads. There are quite a few narrow roads in Scotland, so be aware of this if you have a larger campervan.

SAFETY

Scotland is a beautiful place, but it is infamous for its rapidly changing weather. What might start out as a shorts and t-shirt kind of day can quickly turn into a full-blown winter storm. Remember that, although the hills you are heading up might be smaller than those in mainland Europe, they are still high and very exposed to the elements.

Always pack with safety in mind, especially in any months which have an 'r' in them. Take an extra layer and a waterproof, as well as an emergency blanket at a minimum, plus some emergency rations in case a short day becomes much longer. From September to March, it is also best to take a head torch – just in case.

Even if you have a GPS device with you, always take a paper map and a compass and have the skills to use them. Some of the routes have a shorter option provided in the text, but always have a plan B if things change and you want to cut your run short.

IN THE EVENT OF AN ACCIDENT

If you do require emergency assistance, dial **999** or **112** and ask for the **Police** and then **Mountain Rescue**. Make sure you are able to tell the call handler where you are either using map coordinates or using an app on your phone. If you have intermittent phone signal, an SMS message may send when a call will not connect.

Remember, you will at times be heading into remote areas which can take a long time for emergency services to access, so you will need those extra layers and an emergency blanket. More information can be found at **www.mountaineering.scot**

WEATHER AND AVALANCHE

As I mentioned above, Scotland is infamous for its constantly changing weather. Thankfully, there are a number of excellent resources at your fingertips to keep you informed.

The Mountain Weather Information Service provides simple information to keep you safe in the UK hills. Broken down regionally, you will find information on rain, wind, visibility and temperature: **mwis.org.uk**

Scotland in winter can be fierce, but also beautiful. If you do find yourself heading to Scotland in winter, it is good to understand the risk of avalanches. The Scottish Avalanche Information Service provides the details you need to stay safe in winter, with an avalanche forecasting system for popular areas. There is also an app available to download: **www.sais.gov.uk**

MIDGES AND TICKS

Midges are the necessary evil of enjoying the outdoors in Scotland. These are tiny insects that come out in summer, nibbling you and causing impromptu dances around the tent as people attempt to avoid them. Thankfully, all they cause is a bite and irritation, so I recommend some insect repellent and a midge-net to keep them off.

Ticks, on the other hand, can be problematic. Ticks are small, blood-sucking insects that tend to emerge in late spring and can hang around until late autumn. They look like tiny beetles, with a round body, small head and grippy legs. Ticks can carry Lyme disease – a particularly debilitating disease if not treated.

After each run, check yourself (and your pals) for ticks. Don't be shy, they can hide anywhere! Ideally remove them with a tick remover, or a pair of tweezers. Look out for a red 'bullseye' mark that can appear on the body after a tick bite. This can be an early sign of Lyme disease and you should seek medical attention as soon as possible: **www.lymediseaseaction.org.uk**

Map key

 Route line

 Start

 Route marker

 Route direction

HISTORY, NAMES AND LANGUAGE

As you go through this book and explore Scotland generally, you will probably come across some words that are hard to pronounce, and some that aren't even English at all.

Scotland has a rich language history, the most prominent in this book being Scots Gaelic. Originating in Ireland, Scots Gaelic (*Gàidhlig*) was widely spoken in the Scottish Highlands (the *Gàidhealtachd*, 'the Gaelic lands') and much of Scotland, but it faded as conquests brought new languages into the kingdom. Over the centuries it retreated to the Highlands due to the language being outlawed and its speakers being persecuted, particularly after the Jacobite rebellions in the eighteenth century. It further diminished due to the Highland Clearances of the nineteenth century, when many families were forced from their homes and had to seek a new life in places including Ireland and North America.

Fortunately, efforts are being made to salvage Scotland's language history, and many of the places in Scotland are still known by their Gaelic names.

Here are some handy words to help you get by as you use this book and explore Scotland.

Hills
beinn	hill
buachaille	shepherd
càrn	pile of stone
cruach	round hill, stack
maol	a bare hill
meall	lumpy, round hill
mullach	top, summit
sgùrr	pointed or craggy peak
spidean	pinnacle
stac	cliff
stob	protrusion or lumpy hill
stùc	pinnacle, peak

Features
abhainn	river
allt	stream
aonach	ridge, upland
bealach	pass, col or saddle
ceann	head, headland
coire	corrie
creag	crag, cliff
druim	ridge
eas	waterfall
eilean	island
gleann	narrow valley, glen
inbhir	place of meeting of rivers
loch	lake, fjord
lochan	small lake
rubha	headland, promontory
sròn	nose

Colours
bàn, fionn	fair coloured
buidhe, bhuidhe	yellow
dearg	red
geal	white
glas	grey, green
gorm	blue, green
liath	grey
odhar	dun-coloured
ruadh	red, brown
uaine	green

Description
beag	little
breac	speckled, spotted
caol	slim
fada	long
garbh	rough
meadhan	middle
mòr	large, great
sean	old
ùr	new

Animals
damh	stag
each	horse
eun	bird
fiadh	deer
gobhar	goat
iolaire	eagle
laoigh	calf

Trees
beithe	birch
craobh	tree
chaorainn	rowan
darach	oak
feàrna	alder
giuthas	pine

OPPOSITE *ALPINE-LIKE CAIRNGORM TRAILS* (ROUTE 11)

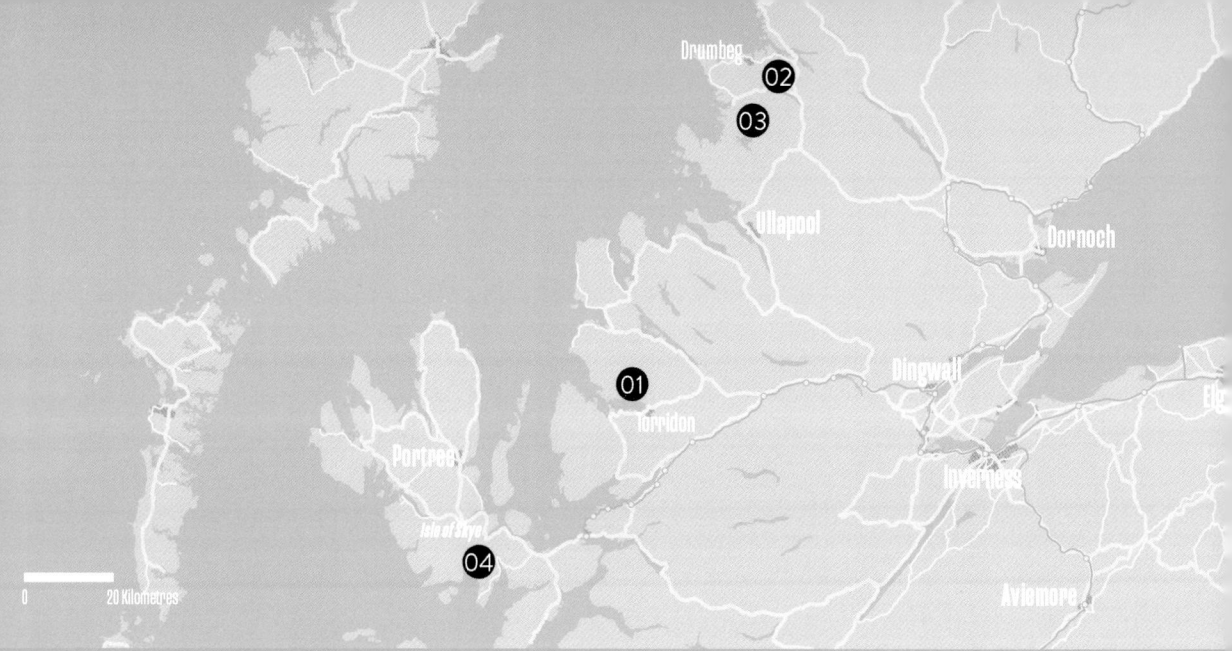

This is an ancient land. Here, some of the oldest rocks in the world can be found, with grumbling mountains seemingly still emerging from the last ice age.

The North West Highlands encompass the wild lands of Assynt, Sutherland, Wester Ross and part of Caithness. It contains some of Scotland's last remaining wilderness, and some of its most remote Munros, such as the Fannichs and the Fisherfield Munros. It is also home to some of the best rock climbing in the country, with the Torridon hills of Beinn Eighe and Liathach famous for their scrambling and steep cliffs.

In recent years, the North Coast 500 has made the area busier, with all the pressures that come from increasing tourist numbers. However, it remains a resolutely rural place, with small towns and shops that close at odd hours, and 'main roads' with just one lane.

It is also a solemn place. The glens were not always this quiet. Not just this area but the whole of the Highlands were witness to the Highland Clearances in the eighteenth and nineteenth centuries, when people were moved off the land to make way for sheep and deer.

I have never quite put my finger on how this landscape makes me feel: it is wonder and awe, but also an awareness of how wild it can be here, especially in bad weather, and how insignificant I am compared to these ancient hills.

Part of that wildness comes from the ever-present Atlantic Ocean, whose depths provide some exquisite local seafood that you find throughout this area. There are also plenty of secluded beaches to discover after a day running around the mountains.

To give you a picture of all this region has to offer, the routes in this book cover a wide area, featuring Torridon's dramatic ridges, a windswept peak on the Isle of Skye, the unique geology of Quinag and the iconic Suilven. Naturally, there is lots to explore beyond these too.

OPPOSITE *NEARING THE SUMMIT OF SGÙRR NA STRÌ* (ROUTE 04)

NORTH WEST HIGHLANDS

'I may be biased, but the north-west coast of Scotland is one of the most scenic areas in the world. Beinn Alligin offers breathtaking views of the other Torridon Munros and across the sea to the islands of Rassay and Skye. On a nice day, you can see the Cuillin mountain range and even out to the Outer Hebrides.' DONNIE CAMPBELL

Donnie is one of Scotland's top mountain runners and coaches, with an incredible racing *palmarès*. In 2020, he set the record for the fastest time to summit each of Scotland's 282 Munros – in just 31 days and 23 hours.

01
BEINN ALLIGIN
10km

As you drive from the south towards the village of Torridon, you will come to a large lay-by overlooking the beautiful sea loch of Upper Loch Torridon. Straight ahead of you sit the majestic and formidable peaks that act as the guardians to this small village. Beinn Alligin (Jewelled Mountain) sits directly opposite, its three horns immediately recognisable. To the right are the jagged spires of Liathach (The Grey One), looming like an enormous castle.

The three Torridon mountain ridges of Beinn Alligin, Liathach and Beinn Eighe (File Mountain, due to its sharp edges) are magnificent playgrounds. Beinn Eighe sees runners taking part in the infamous Celtman Extreme Scottish Triathlon scale its sides on a gruelling marathon, after swimming in jellyfish-infested waters and a 200-kilometre bike ride.

Beinn Eighe is also home to the UK's oldest nature reserve, featuring an area of ancient Caledonian pine forest. If you're in the area, head to Kinlochewe and go for a walk around the reserve. Torridon is rich in wildlife – keep a look out for golden eagles that nest in the crags of Liathach, or even sea eagles.

The run over Beinn Alligin's two Munros – Sgùrr Mòr and Tom na Gruagaich – takes in a fine, grassy saddle, with unbeatable views over its neighbouring peaks and the Atlantic Ocean. The route is circular and can be done either clockwise or anticlockwise. Both are excellent; the directions and GPX file describe the anticlockwise version. It is mostly on trails or rocky ground, with the saddle (bealach) a little grassier.

Distance 10km **Ascent** 1,216m **Time** 3–5 hours **Start** Beinn Alligin car park **Start latitude/longitude** 57.5590, -5.5640 **Start grid reference** NG 869577 **Difficulty** 3/5 – Some light scrambling and exposure, but a manageable day out **Bogs** 1/5 – Not many bogs about up here! However, you can see lots from the top **Terrain** Paths, trails and rock **Map** Harvey Superwalker, Torridon (1:25,000)

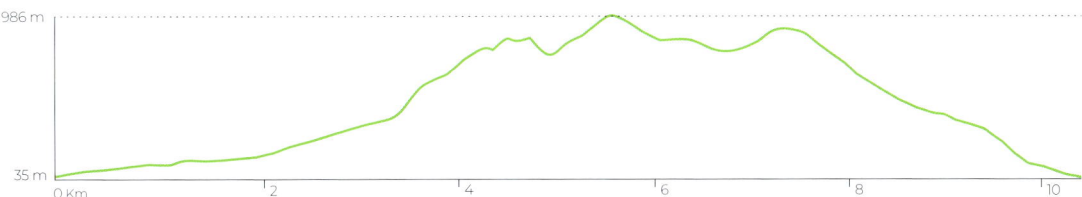

OPPOSITE *VIEW FROM THE SUMMIT OF BEINN ALLIGIN*

DIRECTIONS

S Leave the car park and turn right along the road, cross the bridge then turn left, following a Scottish Rights of Way Society signpost to *Coire Dubh* (Black Corrie). This path is particularly stunning; it can be followed all the way around the northern side of Liathach to the car park at its base. As you make your way along the path, take time to marvel at the old pines to your left, which eventually make way to birch trees. Ahead, the Corbett Beinn Dearg (Red Hill) can be seen, with Beinn Alligin and its distinctive horns on the left. Continue following the river, leaving the woodland behind.

2 After 2km, the path forks (the right fork continues on around the northern side of Liathach while the left fork begins the climb up Beinn Alligin). Take this left-hand fork, following the smaller river. The climbing proper now starts. Cross the river and keep heading towards the prominent rocky buttress up ahead.

3 Keep left at a faint split in the path. What comes next is some exciting but manageable scrambling. Once you have made your way up the face, you will reach another flat section with a big cairn and a great view up to the Horns of Alligin.

4 The path forks and you have a choice: fork right to go up and over the horns or fork left on to a bypass path. When I did it, I went around the side, more because I was in a hurry to get back for a hot chocolate than anything! The horns (which is the route marked on the map and in the GPX file) are straightforward enough – just some extra climbing! As for the 'bypass' route, what it lacks in ascent it makes up for in excitement. The bypass is a narrow trail, skirting the mountainside, with quite an exposed drop on your left. It is still possible to run it, as there aren't any particularly scary parts that require scrambling, but just take care on one or two sections where there is some smooth rock on the path. Either way, you still get amazing views.

ABOVE *VIEW TOWARDS LIATHACH* **BELOW** *LIATHACH AND UPPER LOCH TORRIDON*

ABOVE *BYPASS PATH BELOW HORNS OF ALLIGIN* **BELOW** *HORNS OF ALLIGIN AND LIATHACH*

THE SECOND SUMMIT

The bypass path gives a cracking view to the first summit ahead, with the ridge line elegantly snaking up towards it.

❺ Once you are over the horns (or through the bypass), make the final ascent up Sgùrr Mòr and take it all in! This is probably one of the most remarkable views I have ever seen. I have written a lot in this book about how amazing the Scottish landscape is, and it is not without reason. Now, this all hinges on you being able to see something. If you can't, then you must come back. Once you have filled your phone's memory with photographs (or quietly stored them in your brain), follow the path heading south-west. The mountain's character now changes. After the steep, rough and, at times, airy climbing, the ridge becomes softer and grassier.

❻ You might notice, as you drop into the bealach, that there is a lot of rope strewn across the hillside. From what I have read, this appears to be a historic attempt to stop erosion of the hill's soil – a sign that erosion and environmental damage is not a new thing. The path slowly bends to point south at the bottom of the bealach, starting to climb again towards the summit of Tom na Gruagaich. Make your way over the large boulders that litter the path up the ridge, which flattens out slightly to keep giving awesome views to the summit (trust me, it is getting closer). Continue climbing on a very good path all the way to the summit at 922m.

❼ Once you have spent some time at the summit with its large cairn, head in a westerly direction towards a very shallow bealach. Once there, turn left (south) to reach the head of a steep gully. The gully is stepped almost the entire way; it descends steeply down with steep crags rising high on either side. You get a really ace view down to where you started the route, near the shore of the loch. Strangely, OS paper maps don't show this very obvious path down the hill, whereas Harvey maps do. Keep descending, heading south-south-east; the path eventually joins a thin patch of trees and undergrowth. A few steps later, and you pop out right across from the car park, ready to head off for the next adventure.

BEINN ALLIGIN

POINTS OF INTEREST
- **Munro** Sgùrr Mòr (Big Peak), 986m
- **Munro** Tom na Gruagaich (Hill of the Damsel), 922m

HIGHLIGHTS
- Horns of Alligin
- Airy heights of the bypass route
- Views from Sgùrr Mòr and Tom na Gruagaich
- The beautiful woodland at the start and end of the route

GETTING THERE
There are no practical public transport options for this route.

The car park is located on the road heading west out of Torridon village. Around 4 kilometres after the village you cross a stone bridge; the car park is on your left just afterwards. (The road continues on towards Diabaig, which is excellent for climbing.)

TOP TIP
Don't be fooled by the distance. It may be 'only' 10 kilometres but there are over 100 metres climbed per kilometre in this run and there are some steep ascents and descents to be covered.

OTHER OPTIONS
The Corbett next to Beinn Alligin, Beinn Dearg, is an understated mountain among its larger neighbours. Following the trail to the foot of Beinn Alligin, go left as though heading up to Beinn Alligin. Where the trail forks, bear right, going into Bealach a' Chòmhla. Beinn Dearg is along a stunning ridge with some tricky boulders that require attention (15km; 1,008m ascent).

If you haven't brought your hill legs today, don't worry about it. The trail around the Diabaig peninsula makes for a fun day out. Diabaig is home to some great climbing, too! Starting from Alligin Shuas, follow the shoreline around to Diabaig. The return is on and off the road at times, but is a great alternative day out (12km; 569m ascent).

WHERE TO REFUEL
It would be a crime to go to Torridon and not visit the **Wee Whistle Stop Cafe**, which is inside the Loch Torridon Community Centre. The cafe is community-run, with local people bringing their own recipes and hospitality with them. The scones, which are often accompanied by homemade jam, are incredible.

LOVED THIS ROUTE?
Much of this area is owned by the National Trust for Scotland; learn more at **www.nts.org.uk**

'Quinag sits in the heart of Assynt's unique wild landscape, with views of higher ground one way and the rugged Atlantic Coast the other. This makes it feel much bigger than the map, or your legs, would suggest! A quality mountain day, full of surprises.'   IAN STEWART

Ian is a mountaineering instructor and running guide. He has completed all 282 Munros, won the Cape Wrath Ultra in 2021, and linked all 58 Munros in the Cairngorms National Park in under six days in his 'Cairngorm Parkrun'.

02 QUINAG – THREE CORBETTS *14km*

I remember the first time I visited Achmelvich Beach: as I looked east towards the Assynt mountains I thought they looked like massive guardians to the North West Highlands (swimming in the ice-cold Atlantic Ocean can do that to you). The peaks of Suilven, Cùl Mòr, Cùl Beag and Quinag stand like ships left behind by the receding tide, each spaced evenly apart and surrounded by tundra-like wetlands.

Quinag (*A' Chuinneag* in Gaelic, meaning the Milking Pail) is a beautiful and intriguing mountain range. Shaped like a giant hoof, it features three Corbetts (hills between 2,500 and 3,000 feet (762 and 914 metres) in height, with a prominence of 500 feet (152 metres)), connected by a series of exciting ridges which offer ace views across the North West Highlands and out to the Atlantic. Two of Quinag's three summits – Sàil Gharbh and Sàil Ghorm – allude to its peculiar shape: the Rough Heel and the Blue Heel respectively.

The route begins initially on a very good path, which fizzles out a bit over the slabs as you ascend Spidean Còinich (Mossy Peak), following cairns to the summit. From there, a good trail connects the three tops, with a final descent which is at first boggy before becoming a good path again. The John Muir Trust are undertaking path upgrades from the A894 all the way to Lochan Bealach Cornaidh. Avoid cutting across the fragile peatland and stick to the paths where possible to protect the soil.

Keep an eye out for birds such as ptarmigan, meadow pipit and wheatear while you are out, and marvel at the fact the rock at the base of Quinag is some of the oldest in the world – it is around three billion years old.

Distance 14km **Ascent** 1,065m **Time** 3–5 hours **Start** Quinag car park **Start latitude/longitude** 58.1999, -5.0084 **Start grid reference** NC 233274 **Difficulty** 2/5 – Steep ground in parts and some easy ridge running **Bogs** 2/5 – Very little for much of the run, but can be boggy on the return section **Terrain** Mixture of good paths, off-path sections and bog **Map** Harvey British Mountain Map, Assynt & Coigach (1:40,000)

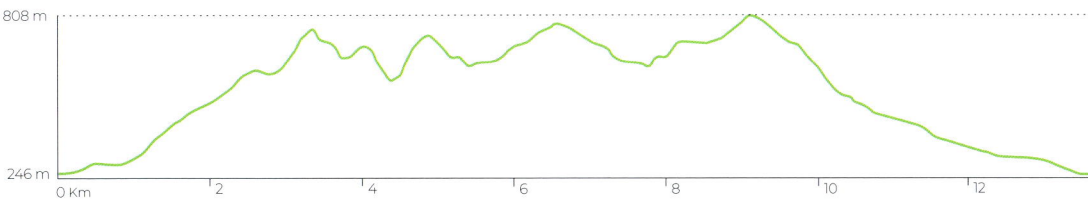

OPPOSITE *THE RIDGE OFF SPIDEAN CÒINICH*

DIRECTIONS

S From the car park, cross the road on to a gravel path. After 500m, at a cairn, the path forks. Take the left-hand path, which soon joins the sweeping arm of the mountain range. The path becomes patchy as you climb – it takes you up a series of stone slabs that can often be more like a riverbed than a path. As you can tell from the photographs, we chose to do this on (initially) a grey and misty day, so the rivers were up and cloud down. Low cloud can make navigation tricky; however, if you keep the steep edge on your right, and continue heading in a westerly direction, you should see a number of small cairns leading you up the hill. On a good day, you will be able to see Spidean Còinich ahead of you, your first peak of the day.

2 After 2.7km, the climbing eases as you reach a flat top (this is not the summit, trust me). Descend slightly over rough ground and the path will appear clearly again. It then climbs steeply up the final ascent to the summit of Spidean Còinich (764m). From here, the views are truly staggering. To the west, you will see your first ridge below you, beyond which stretches the Atlantic Ocean. Looking north, your next two peaks – Sàil Gharbh and Sàil Ghorm – act as the foreground to the wilds of the North West Highlands. To the south, you can marvel at the whale-shaped figure of Suilven and its neighbours, Cùl Mòr and Cùl Beag.

3 As you descend Spidean Còinich, you will join the finest ridge of the day, which eventually descends into Bealach a' Chornaidh. Watch your footing as you descend into the bealach, as some of the rocks can be quite loose. Beyond the bealach, the path climbs steeply again. Behind you, the cragged summit of Spidean Còinich looks seriously impressive, looming over Lochan Bealach Cornaidh.

4 At the top of the climb, you will see the sweeping arm out to Sàil Gharbh on your right, where you will be heading later. For now, descend over the

HEADING BACK TOWARDS SPIDEAN CÒINICH

SPIDEAN CÒINICH VISIBLE ON THE CENTRE LEFT

HEADING BACK TO THE START

slightly rough ground into a dip, in which are some exciting rock formations that you might fancy a shot at standing on to feel the empty air beneath you! It is lots of fun. Skirt along the edge of the hillside in a north-westerly direction on a well-worn path that slowly ascends again. Soon, the path bends to head north with a final climb on to the summit of Sàil Ghorm.

❺ Once you have finished marvelling at the view, retrace your steps back to the dip with the exciting rock features, and begin the ascent back up the slightly rough ground. After 500m, at an elevation of around 700m, turn left on to a path which takes you over to the next arm of the range that leads to Sàil Gharbh. Keep heading east over easy, flat ground before the path slowly curves to the north-east and takes you over a fun boulder field which leads to the summit.

❻ Now, it is time to descend. Retrace your steps down the boulders. Once you are around 500m from the summit of Sàil Gharbh, a small cairn marks the point where you leave your outward route and curve to the left, heading down a faint path which turns into a set of steps. You are now dropping back into Bealach a' Chornaidh.

❼ At the bottom of the steps, keep left and join a muddy path heading directly south-east towards the start of the route. Pass Lochan Bealach Cornaidh on your right, and marvel at the impressive peak of Spidean Còinich. We ran this on a 'dreich' (Scots for damp and overcast) day, so the bogs were quite muddy and wet. The path is constantly improving, so this will become clearer over time. Continue on the path until you reach the road again.

ABOVE *SÀIL GHORM*   LEFT *FOLLOWING THE RIVERBED ON THE FIRST CLIMB*   BELOW *NEAR THE SUMMIT OF SPIDEAN CÒINICH*

POINTS OF INTEREST
- **Corbett** Spidean Còinich (Mossy Peak), 764m
- **Corbett** Sàil Ghorm (The Blue Heel), 776m
- **Corbett** Sàil Gharbh (The Rough Heel), 808m
- **Range** Quinag (The Milking Pail)

HIGHLIGHTS
- Dramatic ridge from Spidean Còinich
- Views over the Atlantic Ocean
- Views across the wilds of Assynt
- Challenging but achievable day out

GETTING THERE
There are no practical public transport options for this route. The Quinag car park sits on the A894, halfway between the junction with the A837 close to Ardvreck Castle and Unapool.

TOP TIP
Quinag's proximity to the sea means it can see some amazing cloud inversions.

OTHER OPTIONS
To shorten the route, Follow the main route over Spidean Còinich and down into Bealach a' Chornaidh. Instead of climbing again, turn right towards Lochan Bealach Cornaidh. Join the path back to the start (8km; 574m ascent).

WHERE TO REFUEL
Need to refuel after your adventure? I highly recommend the pies from **Lochinver Larder**. If it can be in a pie, they will have it – everything from local beef and venison to veggie options. They have some sensational cakes too.

LOVED THIS ROUTE?
Quinag is under the care of the John Muir Trust; learn more at **www.johnmuirtrust.org**

'I've been up Suilven from all four sides, summer and winter; I've run round it, traversed its crest, and climbed it by the crags of Caisteal Liath's nose. Suilven never disappoints. And each time I reach its summit I gaze over the vastness of Assynt and am awed by the drama of this landscape.' ALEC KEITH

Alec is an Inverness-based runner and member of Hunters Bog Trotters. He has been running in Scotland since the mid-1980s and has gone on to race many of the classic Scottish hill races and rounds, including a Ring of Inverpolly in Assynt, taking in Cùl Mor, Cùl Beag, Ben More Coigach, Sgùrr an Fhìdhleir, Stac Pollaidh, Suilven and Canisp.

03 SUILVEN
20km

Suilven is one of the most recognisable peaks of the Scottish Highlands. Its humpback-whale shape is visible for miles around and is often the poster summit for the North West Highlands. The top is only 731 metres above sea level, but it dominates the skyline of Lochinver.

You might look at the landscape around Suilven and think you have been transported to Norway, and you wouldn't be talking total nonsense. This land shares a very similar climate with Nordic countries, so much so that the Vikings found a home-away-from-home when they landed here over 1,000 years ago. The name Suilven illustrates this history – it is from the Norse name *sula* meaning 'pillar' and the Gaelic word *bheinn* (pronounced 'ven') meaning 'mountain'.

I find this area captivating; hence I have also suggested a route around Quinag (pages 9–13), which is a close neighbour of Suilven. The huge bogs surrounding Suilven and Quinag are part of the puzzle in how we tackle the climate emergency. Scottish peatlands store 1.7 billion tonnes of carbon, which is equivalent to 140 years' worth of Scotland's greenhouse gas emissions. For years, peatlands have been drained for forestry, farming and fuel, but many of those in Assynt remain intact.

The route up Suilven is straightforward, but it makes a wonderful adventure. You will see from the photos that we camped on the ridge, which is a great way to experience the Scottish outdoors, particularly in the autumn when you are woken up by roaring stags in the glens! If you do decide to camp, please adhere to the Scottish Outdoor Access Code (page XII). Basically – leave no trace.

Distance 20km **Ascent** 812m **Time** 4–6 hours **Start** Lay-by on minor road east of Lochinver **Start latitude/longitude** 58.1462, -5.2180 **Start grid reference** NC 107220 **Difficulty** 2/5 – Straightforward track in with a steep climb to the bealach **Bogs** 1/5 – Almost entirely dry **Terrain** Excellent track to the foot of the hill and a good path on the summit **Map** Harvey Superwalker, Suilven (1:25,000)

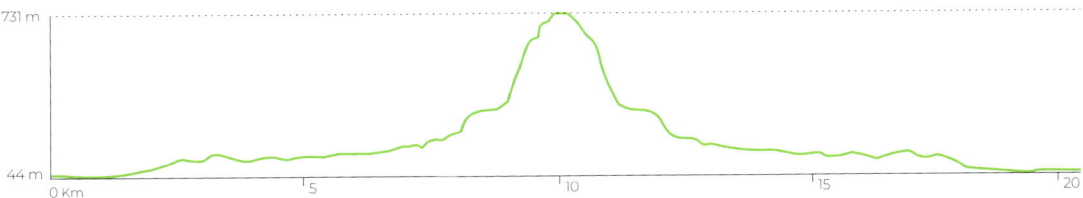

OPPOSITE *HEADING TOWARDS SUILVEN*

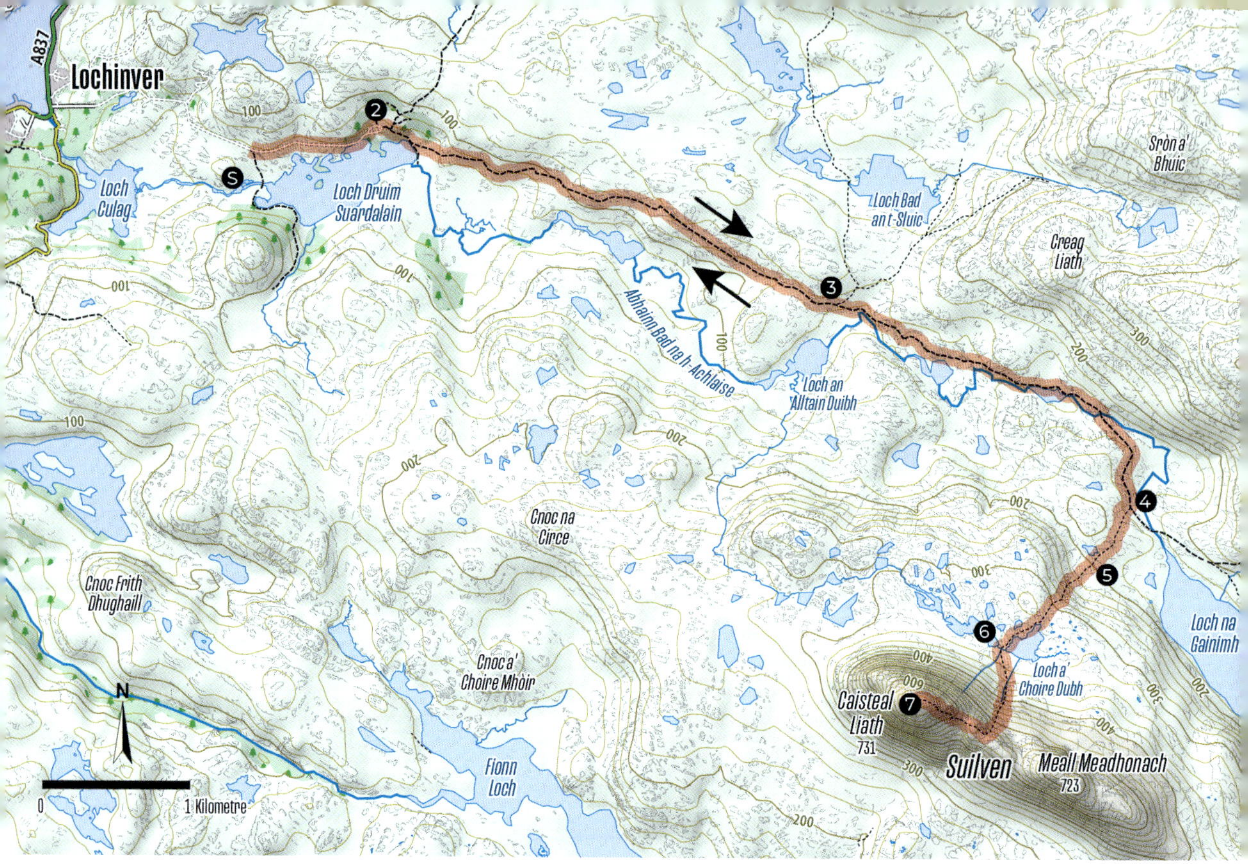

ON THE ROAD BEFORE GLENCANISP LODGE

16 RUNNING ADVENTURES SCOTLAND

SUILVEN FROM THE TRACK

DIRECTIONS

S Run along the tarmac road heading east, eventually coming to the rather grand Glencanisp Lodge, a 12-bedroom Victorian sporting lodge. The building and the estate are now community-owned by the Assynt Foundation, which operates to restore the land through conservation work.

2 Pass the lodge then turn right on to a path, signposted as the *Walker's path to Suilven*. Keep left at a fork and go through a large gate to continue heading east up the glen. Suilven pops in and out of view for a short while before coming to dominate your view on the right-hand side. You now see why I call it a humpback whale? Keep following the rolling quad track, which runs parallel to the river. There are some deep pools that look like cracking swimming spots.

3 Approximately 3.4km after leaving the lodge you reach a junction. (The path on the left goes to Suileag Bothy, which is worth a look.) Keep right to continue on our route, following the main track along the river.

4 Approximately 2.7km after the bothy junction, you will see a clear path, marked by a cairn, leaving the track on the right. Head up this, aiming straight for the mountain. This path – which goes all the way to the bealach – was restored in 2019 in a partnership between the Assynt Foundation and the John Muir Trust.

ABOVE THE FOOTPATH HEADING TOWARDS THE MAIN CLIMB
BELOW THE SUMMIT RIDGE

ABOVE CÙL MOR IN THE DISTANCE **BELOW** CAMPING IN THE BEALACH

CAMPING IN THE BEALACH

Some of the money was awarded to the project through a European-wide online poll, which just shows how much Suilven captures people's imagination. On your left, the landscape opens up to reveal the long Loch na Gainimh.

❺ Begin the steep climb up Suilven's slopes. You will notice a large stone wall ahead of you that drapes the mountain's edges. Therein lies a sinister tale of Scotland's past. In the nineteenth century, during the Highland Clearances, many of those living in the Highlands were forced out of their homes to make way for sheep. Many moved to Australia, Canada and America, but those who were left behind were struck by famine. Some offered themselves to the landowner to build roads and walls in exchange for food. Thus, the 'famine walls' were formed.

❻ If you do intend to camp, get some water before the final climb, as there will be no more available from now on. A final, steep section reveals a precarious-looking boulder, which looks like a seat overlooking the vast landscape. Head up another short climb and you will pop out on the bealach. Turn right to head towards the famine wall, beyond which is the gradual climb to Suilven's main summit – Caisteal Liath (Grey Castle).

❼ This domed summit gives incredible views over the Atlantic in the west and over the vast area of Coigach and Assynt all around you. To return to your start point, simply retrace your steps.

POINTS OF INTEREST
- **Graham** Suilven, 731m
- Glencanisp Lodge
- Suileag Bothy

HIGHLIGHTS
- Superbly runnable trails
- Climbing one of Scotland's most iconic mountains
- The wild landscapes
- Views over the Atlantic Ocean

GETTING THERE
Sadly, the only straightforward way to get to Suilven is by car, although the more intrepid could cycle or kayak! Lochinver lies at the end of the A837; the lay-by at the start of the route is 1.5 kilometres east of the village, along a minor road.

TOP TIP
The parking at the start can be limited – we decided to start later in the day when the mountain would be quieter and then camped near the summit. Alternatively, there is more parking available in Lochinver.

OTHER OPTIONS
Suilven can also be climbed from near Ledmore Junction. Start from the small lay-by on the A835 around 1.5km west of the junction. Head north on a track, following signs for *Lochinver*. Fork right at a junction then turn left to head up Suilven. You can then retrace your steps to Ledmore Junction (28km; 917m ascent) or carry on to Lochinver (25km; 832m ascent).

You can also visit Suilven's lesser-known neighbour Canisp as an out-and-back from the A837 (12km; 728m ascent).

WHERE TO REFUEL
In Lochinver, you cannot go wrong with the **Lochinver Larder**, which sells the best pies in the world – there are plenty of delicious veggie options.

LOVED THIS ROUTE?
The area in which Suilven is situated is managed by the Assynt Foundation. Find out more and donate to their work at **www.assyntfoundation.scot**

'You would be hard pushed to find a more stunning view of the Cuillin mountains and Loch Coruisk than from atop Sgùrr na Strì. Deer roam the steep slopes, sea eagles circle overhead and beautiful floral displays splash the landscape with colour. There really is no better place to enjoy the show than atop the little peak of Sgùrr na Strì.' JORDAN YOUNG

Jordan is a local running and adventure guide with Skye Running Tours and Skye Adventure; he is passionate about being in the mountains and exploring Skye's wild places.

04
SGÙRR NA STRÌ AND CAMASUNARY
23km

Capturing the imagination of people from across the world, Skye, or the Misty Isle, is a beautiful and brutal landscape. A geological jungle, the northern half of the island looks like the remains of a giant's game of Jenga, with huge slabs of volcanic rock frozen mid-tumble along the hills. In the south, jagged peaks strike up to the sky, connected by a snaking dragon's-back of a ridge. At the tip of the dragon's tail lies an isolated little peak, with one of the most stunning views you will find anywhere.

Of all the routes in this book, Sgùrr na Strì was the one I most looked forward to running. Despite its diminutive size of 494 metres, it has an allure far beyond altitude, with a sense of remoteness and stunning scenery.

Often people complete Sgùrr na Strì as an out-and-back from Sligachan. While this is stunning, I wanted to show you more of this fantastic peak and its surroundings.

Starting at Kilmarie, you will approach Camasunary – a truly remote corner of the world where there was once a township of around ten houses. From there you will explore Sgùrr na Strì's eastern corrie before popping out below the summit, from which you will be treated to one of the finest views in the world (in my humble opinion). The way back is on mostly good paths and along the Skye Trail.

Skye is renowned for its wildlife, both on land and in the sea. Golden and white-tailed eagles are common here, as well as many seabirds. Out to sea, whales (including orcas) and dolphins can sometimes be spotted from the shore.

Distance 23km **Ascent** 899m **Time** 3–6 hours **Start** Kilmarie **Start latitude/longitude** 57.1797, -6.0638 **Start grid reference** NG 545172 **Difficulty** 3/5 – Mostly good trails but moderately challenging terrain up to and on Sgùrr na Strì. There is a river to cross which could be challenging after rain **Bogs** 3/5 – Mostly on dry tracks, but Sgùrr na Strì can be waterlogged **Terrain** Mixture of paths, rocky and boggy ground **Map** Harvey Superwalker, Skye: The Cuillin (1:25,000)

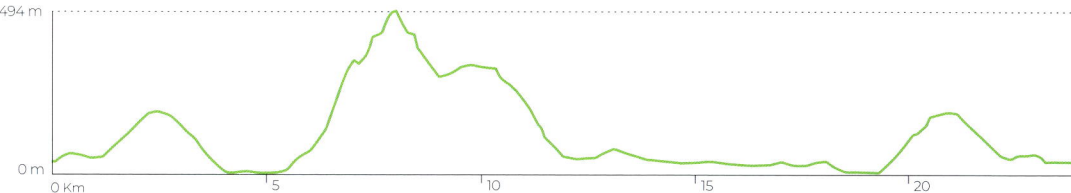

OPPOSITE *RUNNING UP THE ROCKY PATH TOWARDS THE SUMMIT OF SGÙRR NA STRÌ*

LOCH CORUISK

DIRECTIONS

S From the road next to the lay-by, head through the metal gate on to a vehicle track, following signposts to *Camasunary* and *Sligachan*. This track climbs gradually, giving increasingly good views over the sea.

2 After 2.2km, the track levels out and your first amazing view of the day is ahead, with a great perspective over Camasunary and out towards the rolling Atlantic Ocean. Keep following the track as it descends towards the abandoned township. There is a bothy here, which is maintained by volunteers of the Mountain Bothies Association. Despite its beauty, this remote corner of the world is sadly not immune to the pressures of today's world. The beach is covered in marine litter, mostly from the fishing industry. Local volunteers regularly carry out beach cleans here to remove it. Go past the large white building and bear left along a grassy path, after which you will come to a river crossing. If you are here after a period of wet weather, this crossing could be dangerous.

3 Cross the river. Follow the river upstream on a faint stalkers' path, which stays close to the river before taking you further up the hillside. Continue along this (at times) muddy trail, crossing a few small streams. The path bears left and uphill, becoming more defined and following a stream. Where it peters out at 320m above sea level, turn left up a steep gravel path.

4 As the trail flattens out, bear right over boggy ground, then turn left to join the main path up Sgùrr na Strì. Follow the path for 1.2km and keep right as you reach some large boulders. Soon, you will pop out at the cairn and (if it is clear) you will be able to enjoy one of the best views in this book. Overlooking Loch Coruisk, you will see the entire Cuillin Ridge in front of you. Known as the Black Cuillin, this is Britain's answer to alpine climbing. The mountains

THE DESCENT INTO GLEN SLIGACHAN

are comprised of gabbro and basalt, giving them their black colouring, and were formed 60 million years ago from the remains of an enormous volcano. The actual high point of Sgùrr na Strì is on the eastern side, which also affords immense views down to Camasunary and Blàbheinn.

❺ Retrace your steps from the summit and follow the trail downhill. I did this in the rain, and it was surprisingly muddy, so I would recommend some grippy shoes. Keep heading downhill, eventually coming to the edge of a large natural basin. Follow the path around the right-hand side of this, at the opposite side of which you will find a large cairn which marks the descent route into Glen Sligachan. Ahead of you is Marsco and, behind this and to the left, Glamaig, which are part of the Red Cuillin (red due to being made of granite). This is a great path and eventually bottoms out into Glen Sligachan.

❻ After a short while, you will reach a junction. This is where you join the Skye Trail, a 128km trail that goes from the tip to the toe of the island. Turn right at the junction to head back on yourself slightly, following the trail along the edge of Loch an Athain and Loch na Crèitheach. After 6km on this trail, you will be back at Camasunary. Turn left at the white building, cross the bridge and retrace your steps up and over the track, heading back towards Kilmarie. Now, wasn't that an adventure!

POINTS OF INTEREST
- **Summit** Sgùrr na Strì (Peak of Strife), 494m
- Camasunary Beach
- Skye Trail
- Glen Sligachan

HIGHLIGHTS
- Sensational views from the summit of Sgùrr na Strì
- The sense of adventure in this remote and wild place
- Views over Camasunary
- The excellent run along the Skye Trail to finish

GETTING THERE
The route is accessible by bus – the 55 Stagecoach bus runs between Kyle of Lochalsh and Glasnakille, Monday to Friday, with a stop at Kilmarie. Alternatively, if travelling by car, you can park in a long lay-by just beyond Kilmarie.

TOP TIP
There is a river crossing at Camasunary which could be difficult to cross after a spell of wet weather. If this is the case it is likely you will get wet feet, so take waterproof socks if you don't like cold feet!

OTHER OPTIONS
There are lots of trails in this area to choose from. The obvious alternative is to do an out-and-back run to Sgùrr na Strì from Sligachan (23km; 659m ascent).

Alternatively, starting at Kilmarie, you could follow the main route until you reach the descent into Glen Sligachan. Turn left towards Loch Coruisk and either run a lap of the loch (7km; 76m ascent alone) or go back via The Bad Step (21km; 980m ascent).

WHERE TO REFUEL
In Broadford, I would highly recommend **Cafe Sia** and **Siaway**. They have excellent coffee and cake, and even have a wood-fired pizza oven.

If you are sticking around, definitely pay a visit to **Seumas' Bar** at the Sligachan Hotel for excellent local ales and food.

LOVED THIS ROUTE?
This area is looked after by the conservation charity the John Muir Trust. There is a donation tin at the start, or you can donate online **www.johnmuirtrust.org**

THE OLD BOTHY

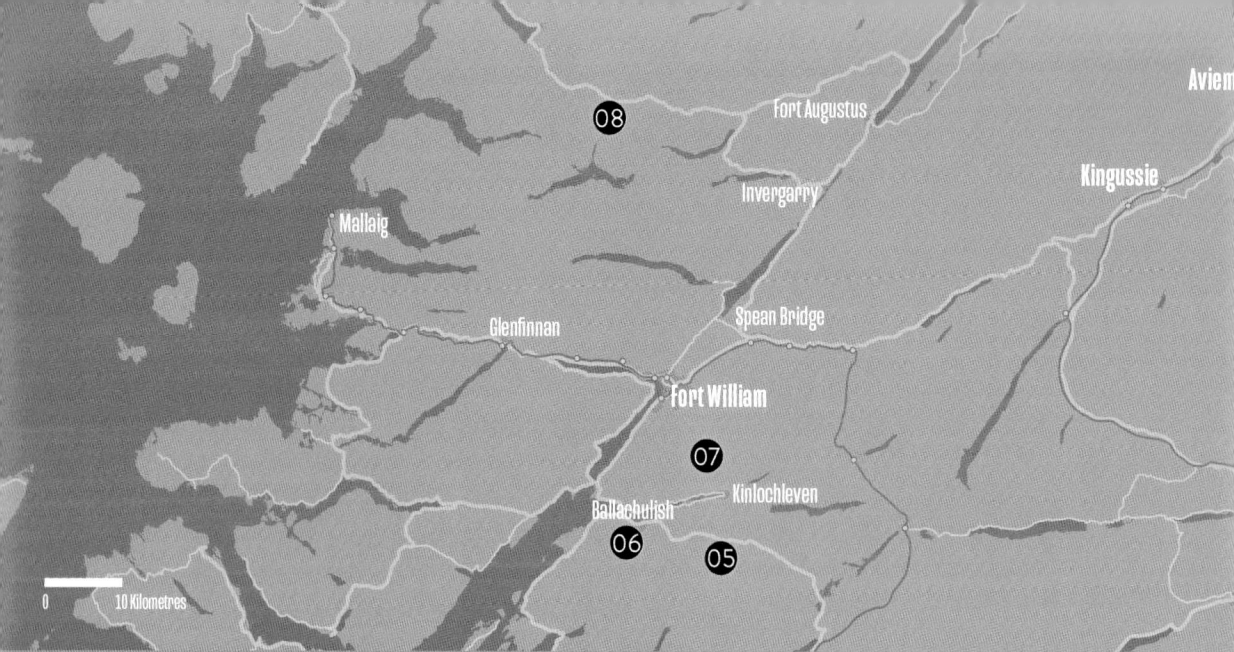

Ask anyone to name iconic Scottish mountains or glens and I can bet most of them will be situated in the Western Highlands: Ben Nevis, the Mamores, Glen Coe, Glen Shiel.

While the Cairngorms are the high arctic plateau, the Western Highlands are the dramatic ridges, steep glens and striking summits. It is here you will find the iconic rounds of Scottish hill running – Tranter's Round, Ramsay's Round, the Etive Round and the Mullardoch Round – along with the end of the West Highland Way and the beginning of the Cape Wrath Trail.

One of Scotland's most iconic hill races, the Ben Nevis Race, takes place near Fort William on the first Saturday of September, where hundreds of runners pitch themselves against this 1,345-metre-high lump, and have done since 1895.

This western part of Scotland was once a stronghold for the Scots Gaelic language. You will notice the road signs changing to reflect this, giving an insight into the old stories of the place. Tyndrum, for instance, was once Taigh an Droma – the house on the ridge.

The Western Highlands are littered with old military roads, which were used by the government to control the Highlands and quash traditional cultures and languages, such as Scots Gaelic, which has long been under threat.

Some of the country's great natural features reside here, such as the vast Rannoch Moor, the magical Steall Falls and remnants of an ancient Atlantic rainforest. Unfortunately, it's also the heartland of the formidable midge, so don't forget your midge spray.

I never tire of running in the Western Highlands, because there's always more to explore. You are spoilt for choice of running routes here – it has everything from towering peaks to wild trails. These routes will take you over dramatic ridges, help you to explore spots less travelled and you'll get to bag a Munro – or seven!

OPPOSITE *MAOL CHINN-DEARG LOOKING TOWARDS AONACH AIR CHRITH (ROUTE 08)*

WESTERN HIGHLANDS

'The Two Lairigs is a classic run in the heart of the Coe with the backdrop and beauty of Glen Coe's higher mountains all around. The place and the views hold many great memories for me. It's truly beautiful and has a mix of everything: trail, spectacular mountain views and the inevitable Scottish bog!' SUZY DEVEY

Suzy is a hill runner living in Lochaber. She is an artist and loves spending time within the local mountain ranges, often working as a guide for Girls on Hills. Her passion is the protection of our natural landscape and environment.

05
GLEN COE'S TWO LAIRIGS
14km

Glen Coe is one of the most spectacular glens Scotland has to offer. If you come from the south, the mountains continue to rise and grow more dramatic, before the big crescendo at the Three Sisters car park.

Glen Coe is the gateway to Lochaber, also known as the Outdoor Capital of the UK, and it's not hard to see why. Everyone from walkers, runners, climbers and cyclists come to this part of the country to experience the incredible landscapes it has to offer.

To the east of Glen Coe is Rannoch Moor, a huge expanse of wetlands and peatbogs; it is an immensely important habitat and helps capture carbon from the atmosphere.

Glen Coe has also hosted a plethora of films and TV series; most notably *Harry Potter and the Prisoner of Azkaban* and the James Bond film *Skyfall*.

For runners, Glen Coe is the site of the Glen Coe Skyline, a 52-kilometre race from Kinlochleven, up Curved Ridge, and along the southern spine of Glen Coe, before taking on the epic ridge line of Aonach Eagach.

While not going up into the mountains, this route gives you a flavour of this sensational landscape on great trails through two quiet glens: Lairig Gartain and Lairig Eilde. Avoid the hustle and bustle and go on a mini adventure to get a feel for the mountains without all the ascent.

Distance 14km **Ascent** 515m **Time** 1.5–3 hours **Start** Glen Coe **Start latitude/longitude** 56.6624, -4.9581 **Start grid reference** NN 188562 **Difficulty** 1/5 – Easy to follow trails and not technical **Bogs** 2/5 – The run along the A82 can be boggy but the rest is on dry trails **Terrain** Generally good paths and trails, with a short section on muddy ground at the turnaround point **Map** Harvey Ultramap, Glen Coe (1:40,000)

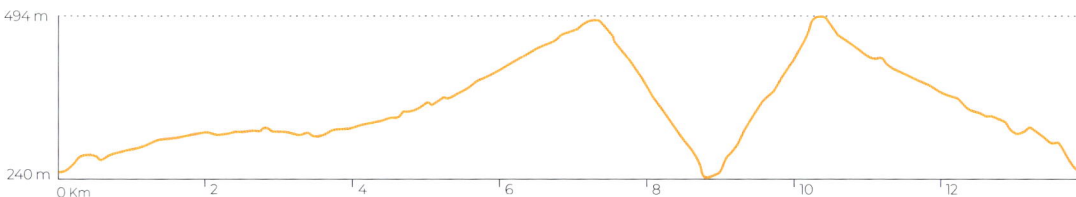

OPPOSITE *RIVER CROSSING NEAR THE END OF THE ROUTE*

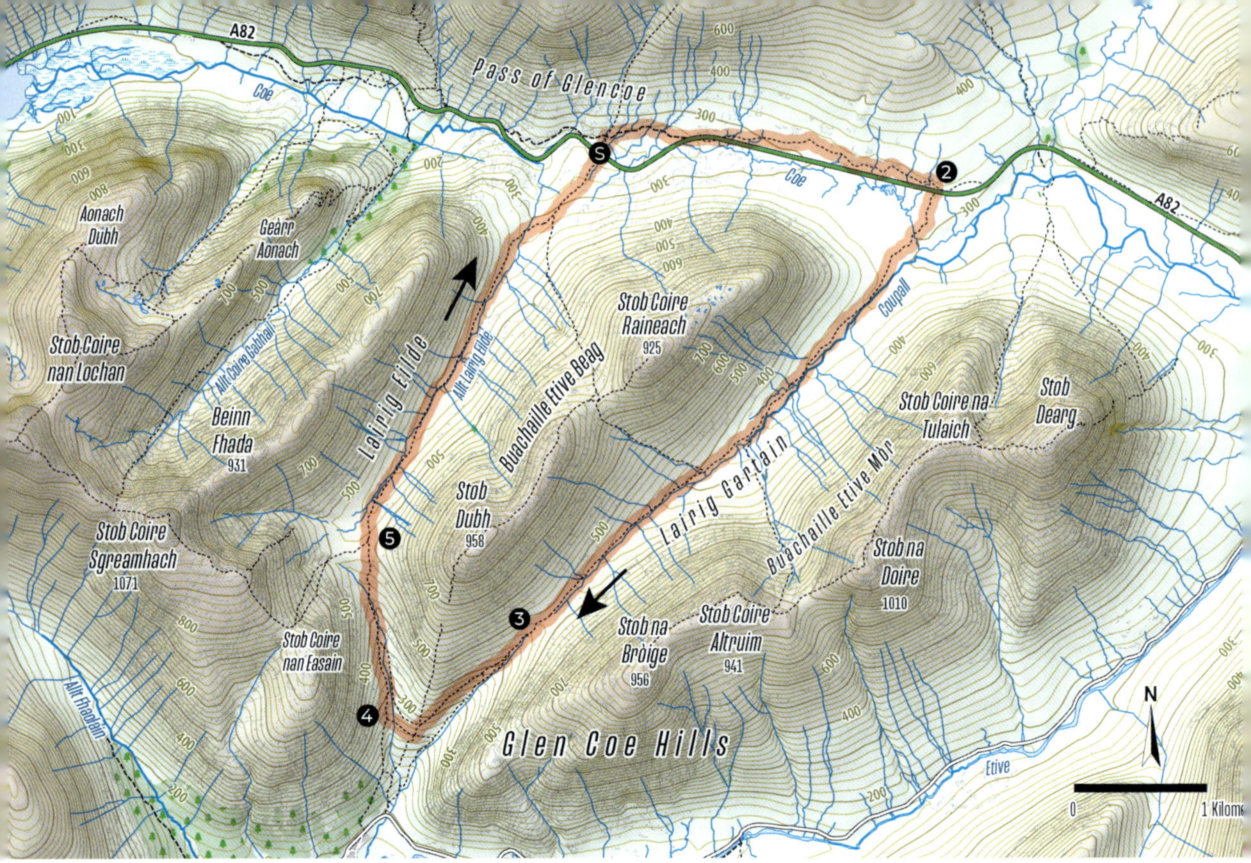

30 RUNNING ADVENTURES SCOTLAND

OPPOSITE *DESCENDING TO GLEN ETIVE* © FINLAY WILD
ABOVE *LAIRIG GARTAIN* **BELOW** *NEAR GLEN ETIVE*

DIRECTIONS

S Cross the busy A82 from the car park and cross the river to the track beyond. This is the old military road that would have been used by government troops to patrol the Highlands during the eighteenth century. Turn right to follow the track alongside the A82, which can be soft and muddy at times. After around 3km leave the track and cross the road to a lay-by, where a signpost indicates *Glen Etive by the Lairig Gartain*.

2 Head up into the glen, with the ridges of Buachaille Etive Mòr and Buachaille Etive Beag rising on either side of you. Follow the burbling river as you climb slowly to a cairn which marks the high point of Lairig Gartain. From here, you can look over Glen Etive, which ends at Loch Etive. Glen Etive sits right at the edge of the ancient Gaelic kingdom of Dál Riata, which, between the fifth and seventh centuries, was a kingdom that spanned from Northern Ireland and encompassed much of Argyll and Bute. It is also what allowed Scots Gaelic to become a dominant language here.

ABOVE *DESCENDING TO GLEN ETIVE* **BELOW** *SIGNPOST*
OPPOSITE *MEMORIAL CAIRN AT THE START OF THE ROUTE*

❸ Descend from the cairn towards Glen Etive. As you drop down, keep an eye on your right for a faint trod. This will take you across the Allt Lairig Eilde, parallel to a high deer fence, and join back on to a path on the opposite side of the water.

❹ Climb steadily, now following the Allt Lairig Eilde, up to another cairn which marks the high point of Lairig Eilde. It's not uncommon to spot large herds of deer in these glens, especially in autumn when the rutting season starts. Scotland has a very high number of deer, which means its landscape has very few trees as saplings are quite attractive to deer. Over the years, deer have lost their natural predators and their numbers have been bolstered to bring income to shooting estates.

❺ Next is a superb descent down Lairig Eilde, at the bottom of which is a short river crossing which can prove tricky if in spate. After that, it's a short jog downhill back to the start of the route.

POINTS OF INTEREST
- Lairig Eilde
- Lairig Gartain
- Glen Etive

HIGHLIGHTS
- Easily accessible from the road
- Great way to experience the mountains without all the climbing
- Great views into Glen Etive
- Superbly runnable trail

GETTING THERE
The 914 Citylink bus runs through Glen Coe. There is no official stop at the start of the route, but you could request it from the driver who may be able to let you off nearby.

Alternatively, there is a car park at the start of the route – it is on the south side of the A82, opposite a large beehive-shaped memorial cairn. Be aware that the traffic during summer months in Glen Coe can be problematic, with large volumes of cars and tour buses. Be mindful of when you travel.

TOP TIP
Be sure to bring a camera – the view down into Glen Etive at the halfway point is unique and beautiful.

OTHER OPTIONS
There are a few alternative routes to choose from. Of course, you could start the route from Glen Etive, as there is a car park near the turnaround point in the glen.

Alternatively, you could ignore the second road crossing at the northern end of Lairig Gartain and instead continue on to the Buachaille Etive Mòr car park. Head up 'The Bookle' (as many call it), include out-and-backs to Stob Dearg and Stob na Bròige, and drop back down to Lairig Gartain to continue on the main route (23km; 1,586m ascent).

Another extension would be to follow the route until point **5**, at which point you could head up to Stob Coire Sgreamhach and down into the Lost Valley (Coire Gabhail), (19km; 1,201m ascent).

LOVED THIS ROUTE?
This area is looked after by the National Trust for Scotland. You can find out more about their work at www.nts.org.uk

WHERE TO REFUEL
To the east of the route, you could go to the **Kingshouse Hotel** for hot chocolate or some food. In the other direction, there is the **Glencoe Cafe** in Glencoe village and the **Quarry Cafe** between Glencoe village and Ballachulish.

'The Ballachulish Horseshoe is often overlooked on account of its proximity to the popular giants of Glen Coe. But it's a significant undertaking (starting from sea level) and its coastal position gives it fantastic views down Loch Linnhe and over the many summits stretching inland as far as the eye can see.' KERI WALLACE

Keri is a fell runner, skyrunner, rock climber and writer. She is Summer Mountain Leader and Rock Climbing Instructor qualified – and a mother of two young children. She has been running and racing in the Scottish mountains for 12 years and lives in Glencoe.

06 BEINN A' BHEITHIR – THE BALLACHULISH HORSESHOE *16km*

Beinn a' Bheithir translates to mean 'Hill of the Thunderbolt', which is as good a reason as any for this epic horseshoe to feature in this book.

On top of its wicked name, the Beinn a' Bheithir range (also known as the Ballachulish Horseshoe) stands mightily above Loch Leven and the little village of Ballachulish, right at the end of the picturesque Glen Coe. If you're coming from the north, your eyes cannot help but be drawn to these towering peaks, which hide a folk tale to match its impressive name.

According to legend, a dragon used to dwell in the corrie of this mountain range, gobbling up passing villagers and pestering the town – a bit like Smaug from *The Hobbit*. One day, the villagers set a trap on the loch with bait, and successfully vanquished the dragon. Little did they know that the dragon's offspring would grow to continue their mother's village-bothering.

Thus far, I haven't come across any dragons on this range, but it would certainly spice things up a bit! However, with stunning views across Glen Coe, Loch Leven, Loch Linnhe and the remote bounds of the Ardnamurchan peninsula, most people will be more than content with what is already there to enjoy.

Of course, there is the Schoolhouse Ridge, which is a phenomenal, easy scramble to make this an epic day in the mountains and make you feel a tiny bit like Kilian Jornet. If scrambles aren't your thing, the steep grassy slope up Beinn Bhàn is also an option. Be aware that the descent is via a working forestry plantation, so there may be diversions or deviations from the route described, and the forest might look quite different as trees are felled.

Distance 16km **Ascent** 1,328m **Time** 3–6 hours **Start** Ballachulish **Start latitude/longitude** 56.6780, -5.1292 **Start grid reference** NN 084584 **Difficulty** 3/5 – Some light scrambling and exposure, with some care needed on rocky sections **Bogs** 3/5 – The start of the final descent is a bit boggy **Terrain** Rocky across the ridge, a short bog, a fire road and tarmac – a bit of everything! **Map** Harvey Superwalker, Glen Coe (1:25,000)

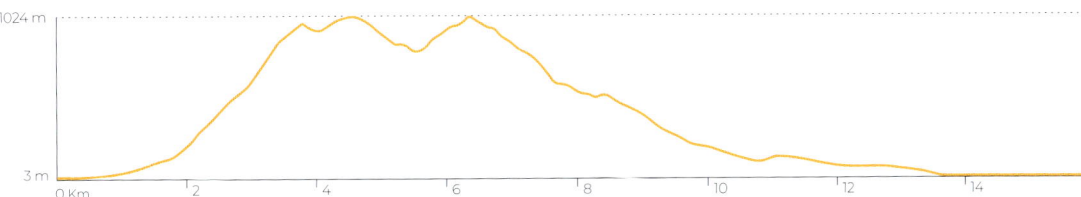

OPPOSITE *ON THE SCHOOLHOUSE RIDGE*

DIRECTIONS

S You will be able to see the impressive spine of the Schoolhouse Ridge from the start of the route. Follow the road into town, keeping left at the fork and heading for the hills. Cross a small bridge then immediately turn left and go past a school. (If you want to avoid the ridge, take a right through the field immediately after the school and climb the steep, grassy slope up Beinn Bhàn. This eventually levels out and heads south to the first top.) For those keen for the ridge, follow the farm track through a series of gates.

2 After about 750m on the farm track, go through another gate and keep an eye out for a small pile of stones indicating the path up to the Schoolhouse Ridge. Turn right on to this path. The initial kilometre is on some pretty soft ground, through heather and bracken (in the summer months). It's a fairly steep climb, so there will be plenty of opportunities to stop and admire the view. After about 350m of climbing, you will meet the ridge. About 500m along it, there is a bit of a 'climb' up a small face. There is a bypass around the base of it if you don't fancy the scramble. Around 200m later, the ridge widens to leave a rocky climb to the summit of Sgorr Bhan, giving sensational views in every direction. Follow the slowly rising ridge up to Sgorr Dhearg, the first Munro of the day.

3 I know – Sgorr Dhonuill looks really far away, but it isn't that bad! Take care as you descend off Sgorr Dhearg, as it is rocky and loose in places – not fun for tired ankles. Halfway into the bealach, the rocks give way to grass before you head steeply up the other side. The path zigzags upwards. In summer, you will see the emerging wild blueberries in the rocky crags; if you are there in late summer, you might even be able to enjoy some of them. A short ridge section follows, after which is the final short dig to the summit of Sgorr Dhonuill. From the top, you can overlook where the land meets the sea, with Loch Linnhe connecting to the Firth of Lorn

ABOVE VIEW OVER LOCH LEVEN
BELOW VIEW TOWARDS THE RIDGE

LEFT THE FIRST SECTION OF TRACK
BELOW LEFT START OF THE SCHOOLHOUSE RIDGE ASCENT
BELOW RIGHT THE RIDGE BETWEEN SGORR BHAN AND SGORR DEARG

VIEW FROM SGORR DHONUILL CLIMB **BELOW RIGHT** *THE RIDGE FROM TOWN*

and, later, the Atlantic Ocean. On a good day, you will be able to see the Isle of Mull and its lone Munro – Ben More.

④ Leave the summit of Sgorr Dhonuill and return to the bealach. Turn left to begin descending. I was here after a couple of days of rain and the paths and grass were quite slippery and boggy, so take your time. Cross a small stream a couple of times then the ground flattens out to become a marshy basin. On your right, you will see a line of fenceposts. Follow these and a faint path as you head towards the plantation.

When I last ran the route, some of the forest had just been felled, so it was a little messy, but there is a clear path along the fence line.

⑤ Enter the forest on some gorgeous singletrack before crossing a forest track on to yet more lovely singletrack. At the second forestry junction, turn right. Follow this forestry track as it heads north and then bends right, running parallel to the road below. Bear left and re-emerge at the road at a big house. Turn right and follow the pavement for the final 2km back to the start.

POINTS OF INTEREST
- Schoolhouse Ridge
- **Summit** Sgorr Bhan (White Peak), 947m
- **Munro** Sgorr Dhearg (Red Peak), 1,024m
- **Munro** Sgorr Dhonuill (Donald's Peak), 1,001m

HIGHLIGHTS
- Easily accessible
- View from first summit to Glen Coe
- View from second summit over the sea
- Enjoyable scramble on Schoolhouse Ridge

GETTING THERE
There is a railway station in Fort William; buses run several times a day from there to Ballachulish.

Alternatively, there is a tourist car park in Ballachulish, beside the little tourist information centre. There is no charge or time limit if you park here.

NOTE
The final descent is through a working forestry plantation. This means that the route is subject to change. Please follow guidance where necessary.

TOP TIP
Obviously, all the routes in this book would be ideal to do on a clear, sunny day, but this one I would absolutely wait for a good day to do. The views into Glen Coe are stunning, and the views across the coast and up to the Lochaber hills are not to be missed.

OTHER OPTIONS
Due to its easy access, you can decide to do one or other of the hills alone. If you only have time or energy for a short but fun day out, head up the Schoolhouse Ridge to Sgorr Bhan and descend via Beinn Bhàn's steep, grassy slope (8km; 921m ascent). Otherwise, you could start in South Ballachulish, head up into the forest and pop up either one or both of the Munros.

WHERE TO REFUEL
Despite its seemingly small size, the visitor centre by the car park is like a Tardis. Inside there is a lovely cafe, which sells some decent sized burgers and what it claims to be the #BestCoffeeInBalla.

'Scotland is home to some of the best mountain territory there is. The Ring of Steall has a great mixture of fast running, rocky scrambling, steep climbs, slippy descents and soaring ridges ... the Mamores have it all!' HOLLY PAGE

Holly is an international trail and mountain runner. She was the second female finisher in the Ring of Steall Skyrace in 2019; she represents England and Great Britain abroad. Holly can often be found in her van in the Scottish Highlands or the Alps, or exploring the world by bike or on foot.

07
RING OF STEALL
17km

The Ring of Steall has for a long time been an iconic walking route but has become increasingly popular with runners, thanks in part to the Ring of Steall Skyrace, but also the growing mountain-running community in Fort William. In the Ring of Steall Skyrace, part of the Golden Trail National Series, runners from across the globe descend on the village of Kinlochleven to run this iconic trail, and it is no wonder they do!

The route I have for you describes the classic version of the route, starting in Glen Nevis. I have graded it as very technical as a heads-up to those uncomfortable on steep, exposed ground. The ridges are challenging for those not used to it.

Up high, you will traverse the famous Devil's Ridge, between Sgùrr a' Mhàim and Sgùrr an Iubhair, as well as the phenomenal ridge between An Garbhanach and An Gearanach. The Devil's Ridge is tamer than its name suggests, but both ridges require care.

The steepness of the climbs means that you will have ample opportunity to catch your breath and look around at the stunning landscape: the humpbacked figure of Ben Nevis and its neighbouring Munros of Càrn Mòr Dearg, Aonach Beag and Aonach Mòr and the long spine of the Grey Corries.

Some of this route, as well as the neighbouring mountains, are the scene of Ramsay's Round – the 24-hour mountain challenge – Scotland's equivalent of the Bob Graham Round.

It's tough to have favourites in this book, but this may be one of mine!

Distance 17km **Ascent** 1,653m **Time** 3–6 hours **Start** Glen Nevis **Start latitude/longitude** 56.7692, -5.0369 **Start grid reference** NN 145683 **Difficulty** 5/5 – Two graded ridges and several sections on steep ground **Bogs** 2/5 – The area around Steall Falls can be very boggy; dry elsewhere **Terrain** Largely rocky ground and trails **Map** Harvey Ultramap, Ben Nevis (1:40,000)

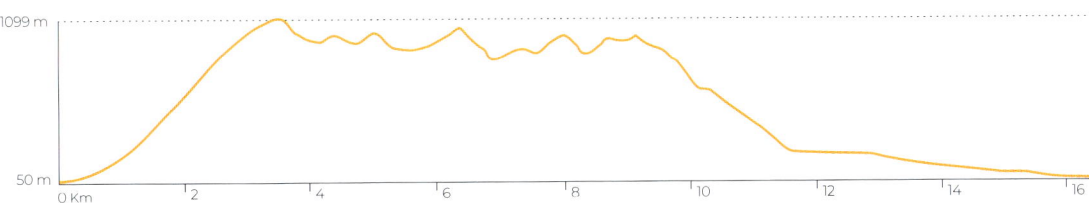

OPPOSITE *THE DEVIL'S RIDGE*

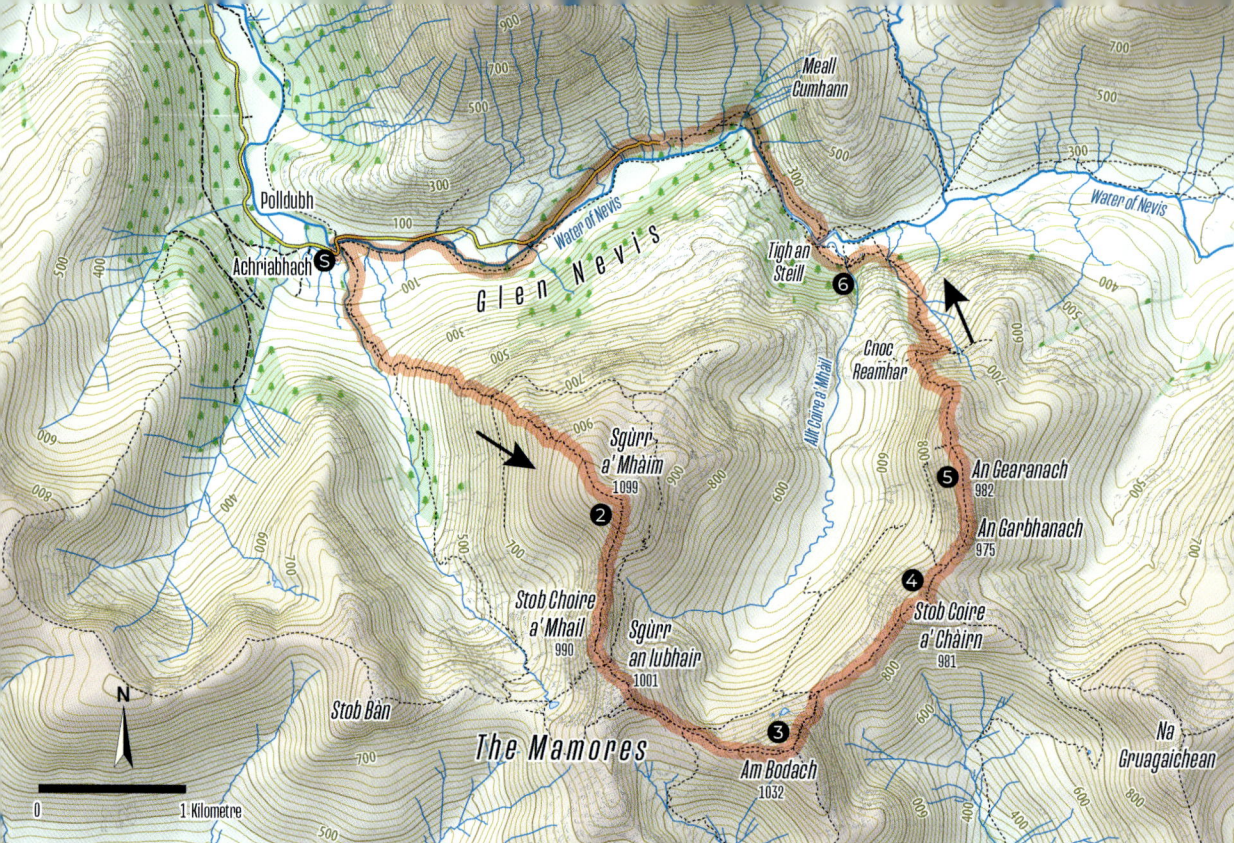

DIRECTIONS

S The route starts from the Lower Falls car park in Glen Nevis. (If starting at the Upper Falls car park, follow the road downhill then turn left on to a trail which crosses a bridge and follows the river downhill.) Leave the car park and turn right, heading towards a bridge over the Water of Nevis. On your right just before the bridge is a trail next to the river up to the upper car park. To the right of this is a track heading south-east towards the slopes of Sgùrr a' Mhàim; follow this track for 1km over a gently rising trail and some bogs before turning up to the left and through a gate. Begin the long climb up your first Munro, Sgùrr a' Mhàim; the path wiggles its way up towards the quartz-topped summit at 1,099m. There is a cracking view to Ben Nevis behind you and a spine-tingling view over the upcoming Devil's Ridge.

2 Head south from the summit of Sgùrr a' Mhàim on to the Devil's Ridge. The Devil's Ridge, despite its name, is not the most formidable of ridges. It is a little exposed in places, requiring some squeezy downclimbs, but is manageable with care. The crux is near the middle, with a short downclimb before popping back up on to the ridge at a narrow point. The ridge broadens and you begin to climb over Stob Choire a' Mhail towards Sgùrr an Iubhair (Sgùrr an Iubhair is no longer part of the exclusive Munro club after it was deemed to be a subsidiary summit). Head south-east from the summit, downhill into a wide bealach which provides some nice running and excellent views south towards Glen Coe and the spiney ridge of Aonach Eagach. Ignoring paths dropping left and right from the bealach, ascend Am Bodach, your second Munro, via a short climb on gently rising ground.

3 Descending Am Bodach is a case of joining up patchy paths down some big boulders. From the top, drop down to the north-east. The boulders eventually give way to easier zigzags on softer ground. In the bealach, follow the path

ABOVE VIEW TOWARDS BEN NEVIS **BELOW** ROCKY GROUND ON THE ROUTE

to the right and up to Stob Coire a' Chàirn, your third Munro, which is a slightly underwhelming peak but gives cracking views of its neighbours – how nice of it.

❹ Now comes the tricky part. Descend steeply downhill in a northerly direction, followed by a steep and slightly eroded uphill climb to An Garbhanach. To get to your fourth and final Munro, An Gearanach, you need to cross a narrow ridge. (It is possible to take an easier line to the right of the ridge, allowing for a bit of a bypass.) The ridge is narrower than the Devil's Ridge, but there is no downclimbing to be done, so that's a plus. Once you are over it, though, An Gearanach feels like you are on the edge of the world; its steep sides making you feel like you are on a huge tower. Don't worry, though, you won't fall off.

AN GEARANACH AND STOB COIRE A' CHÀIRN

5 Continue north over the summit to descend on a meandering trail which flattens out at around 650m altitude. The Ring of Steall race comes up this way and, I have to admit, I really wanted to lie down at this point with a cold beer – it is a fantastic viewpoint towards Ben Nevis and a great picnic spot. Turn right and run along a long terrace. Below you, you can see the path sweeping its way down the hill; turn left to join this path. At the base, descend on some loose gravel to reach the valley floor. Bear left and follow the base of the hill, at which point you will reach the magical Steall Falls on the Allt Coire a' Mhàil – even more magical as this is where they filmed the quidditch scenes in one of the *Harry Potter* films. Though, you'd never know that they'd had a stadium full of wizards there at any point …

6 Cross the Allt Coire a' Mhàil and aim for the small hut beyond (next to the Water of Nevis), which is maintained by the Lochaber Mountaineering Club and can be rented by groups. Cross the Water of Nevis; depending on the river's depth, you may need to cross the wire bridge. If it is low, it's possible to cross at one of the nearby banks. Join the main Steall Falls Path into the trees; it is a nice, fast trail with a few waterfalls crossing the path. At the end of the trail lies the Upper Falls car park; follow the road downhill from here then turn left on to a trail which crosses a bridge and follows the river downhill back to the start of the route.

AM BODACH

POINTS OF INTEREST
- **Munro** Sgùrr a' Mhàim (Peak of the Rounded Hill), 1,099m
- **Munro** Am Bodach (The Old Man), 1,032m
- **Munro** Stob Coire a' Chàirn (Peak of the Corrie of the Cairn), 981m
- **Munro** An Gearanach (The Complainer), 982m

HIGHLIGHTS
- Beautiful Steall Falls
- Two ridges – An Gearanach and the Devil's Ridge
- Incredible views all around
- Exciting terrain in a manageable distance

GETTING THERE
There is a railway station in Fort William; buses run several times a day (from May until October) from Fort William into Glen Nevis, as far as the Lower Falls car park www.shielbuses.co.uk

Alternatively, if you arrive by car, Lower Falls car park is at the start of the route. Upper Falls car park is further up the glen; however, it is small and often busy.

TOP TIP
Water is in short supply up here. If you think you will be out for a long day, be sure to take a little extra, just in case.

OTHER OPTIONS
The Ring of Steall Skyrace starts in Kinlochleven. If you fancy this route, start in Kinlochleven and follow the road heading west. Turn right on to the path signposted *West Highland Way*. Climb until you leave the trees behind. Follow the wide track west for 500m before turning right, alongside the Allt Coire na h-Eirghe.

The path gets steeper, eventually popping out at the foot of Sgùrr an Iubhair. Follow the main route now (in a clockwise direction instead of anticlockwise) over Sgùrr a' Mhàim, round to Stealls Falls, over An Gearanach and back to Am Bodach.

From Am Bodach, drop into the saddle towards Sgùrr an Iubhair and retrace your steps to descend into Kinlochleven (28km; 2,610m ascent).

WHERE TO REFUEL
After a day in the Glen Nevis mountains, absolutely nothing beats the **Ben Nevis Inn**. Right at the foot of Britain's tallest mountain, no one looks out of place here. You can be drenched, sunburnt, in full winter gear or in shorts and you will make friends. The grub is incredible and the atmosphere like that of a classic mountain lodge.

For coffee, **The Wildcat** in Fort William is a superb vegan cafe. Otherwise, try the **Larder Cafe** at the Highland Soap Company on the A82 just north of Fort William.

LOVED THIS ROUTE?
The Steall Falls section of this route is cared for by the John Muir Trust. Learn more at **www.johnmuirtrust.org**

'The South Glen Shiel Ridge proved perfect for the fast start I wanted for my round – easy navigation, good running and paths almost everywhere. The views in all directions are fantastic: the secluded Knoydart and the remote peak of Ladhar Bheinn. Sat among such exalted neighbours, it gives some of the finest ridge running Scotland has to offer.' JON BROXAP

Jon is a retired fell runner who spent his racing career fruitlessly chasing Keswick club mates Billy Bland and Kenny Stuart. In 1988 he climbed 29 Munros in the Kintail–Affric hills in 24 hours, setting a record that stood for 29 years.

08
SOUTH GLEN SHIEL RIDGE – SEVEN MUNROS IN A DAY *27km*

The South Glen Shiel Ridge is a beautiful spine. Seven Munros are linked together on one of the most stunning and enjoyable ridges a runner could hope for.

To the south-west, you are able to see one of the true wildernesses of Scotland – Knoydart. To the north lies the northern Glen Shiel Munros and, beyond that, the stunning Glen Affric; west, and you are looking at Skye.

Glen Shiel is an all-you-can-eat buffet of Munro bagging. On either side of the River Shiel, almost every summit you see is a Munro, connected by a long chain of ridges. On the southern side, from The Saddle to Creag a' Mhàim, there are nine Munros. To the north, from Sgùrr Fhuaran to Càrn Ghluasaid, are another 12.

It is no wonder that, in 1988, Jon Broxap set off from the Cluanie Inn to touch the summits of 29 Munros in under 24 hours, covering a staggering 126 kilometres and over 10,000 metres of ascent, setting a new record in the process.

Long before Jon set off up Creag a' Mhàim on his epic round, Glen Shiel was the scene of another moment in history; this one involving Jacobites, Spanish marines and the British Army. On 10 June 1719, the Jacobite army of Highlanders and

Distance 27km **Ascent** 1,880m **Time** 6–8 hours **Start** Màlagan, Glen Shiel **Finish** Cluanie Inn **Start/finish latitude/longitude** 57.1710, -5.3561/57.1558, -5.1777 **Start/finish grid reference** NG 972139/NH 079117 **Difficulty** 2/5 – It's a long day in the hills, but there is an obvious trail and there is not much technical ground along the ridge **Bogs** 3/5 – The start is quite boggy and, if it has rained a lot, the grassy ridge may be soggy in places; otherwise, quite dry **Terrain** Largely grassy; peppered with rocks **Map** Harvey British Mountain Map, Knoydart, Kintail & Glen Affric (1:40,000)

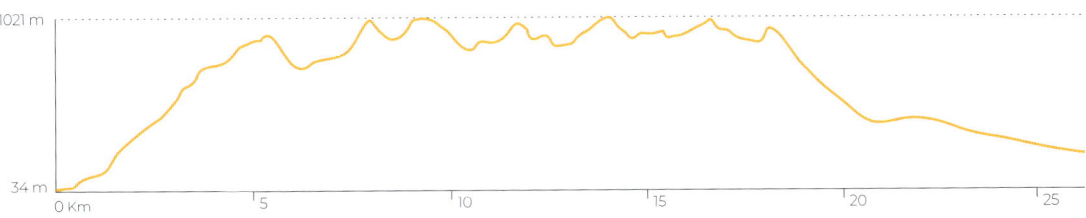

OPPOSITE *LOWER SLOPES OF CREAG NAN DAMH*

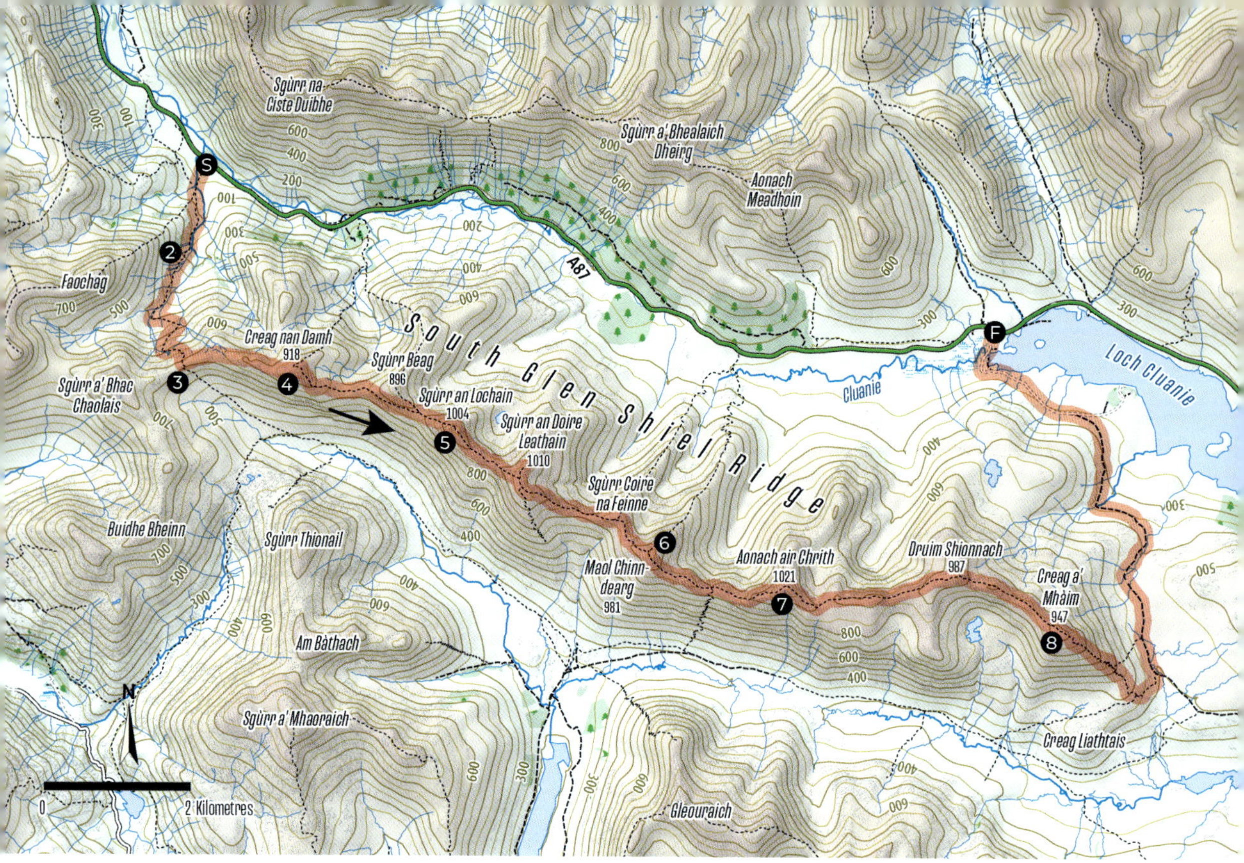

ON THE FIRST CLIMB

Spanish soldiers was defeated by British troops. Near the start of the route, you will see a sign with a pair of crossed swords, indicating the battle site. As a tribute to the Spanish soldiers, there is a peak on the northern ridge called Sgùrr nan Spainteach – Peak of the Spaniards.

Don't get too distracted gazing up to the Peak of the Spaniards or the fearsome Forcan Ridge though, because you might have a close encounter with one of the Glen Shiel feral goats that often frequent the A87.

The route I like best runs west to east. As a point-to-point, you need to consider how to get back to the start of the route. Heading west to east means that, if you are going by bike back to the start of the route, the ride is all downhill – handy after a long day. Plus, the smooth, gradually descending track is (I think) better at the end so you finish with dry feet.

THE WALL RUNNING ALONG THE RIDGE

DIRECTIONS

S Your adventure starts at a gate in the middle of a long deer fence. Beside the gate are signs to *Kinlochhourn, Loch Quoich* and *Tomdoun*. Go through the gate, initially on a grassy track, before starting on a path towards the river. Once you are across the river, follow the path that runs next to the deer fence, heading south. When we were there, the path had been blocked a little by a landslip, so just be careful as you go along.

2 Keep following the river until the path curves to the right, leaving the deer fence behind and climbing more steeply. After a short while, the path levels out and you cross a stream (a burn, as we call them in Scotland), where two other streams meet. From here, you have a great view through to Sgùrr na Sgine. Begin climbing steeply up the zigzag path, continuing to head south, until you pop on to the ridge.

3 You will now find a wall I call the 'Great Wall of Glen Shiel' in front of you. This runs across almost the entire ridge, so you shouldn't find it too hard to follow this route. Turn left from where you emerged and begin climbing slowly in an easterly direction towards the first top, Creag nan Damh. Genuinely, the views from here to Sgùrr na Sgine in the west and Knoydart towards the south are well worth taking stock of. There is a very short bum-shuffle down and steep climb back up before the summit of Creag nan Damh, which requires some care. This is your first summit of the day.

4 Descend on a good path and follow the right fork to skirt the small lump ahead. Climb a little more steeply to the top of Sgùrr an Lochain.

5 The section to Sgùrr an Doire Leathain is straightforward, with just a short out-and-back to the third summit of the day. Here is a true highlight: the view of the ridge dropping east

ABOVE *CREAG NAN DAMH* BELOW *MAOL CHINN-DEARG*

POINTS OF INTEREST
- **Munro** Creag nan Damh (Rock of the Stags), 918m
- **Munro** Sgùrr an Lochain (Peak of the Small Loch), 1,004m
- **Munro** Sgùrr an Doire Leathain (Peak of the Broad Thicket), 1,010m
- **Munro** Maol Chinn-dearg (Bald Red Head), 981m
- **Munro** Aonach air Chrith (Trembling Ridge Hill), 1,021m
- **Munro** Druim Shionnach (Ridge of the Fox), 987m
- **Munro** Creag a' Mhàim (Rock of the Large Rounded Hill), 947m

HIGHLIGHTS
- View from Creag nan Damh towards Sgùrr na Sgine and the Forcan Ridge
- View of the ridge descending Sgùrr an Doire Leathain
- Very runnable terrain with good paths
- Feeling of adventure

GETTING THERE
As I mentioned, this is a point-to-point, so requires a little preparation. The route starts at Màlagan in Glen Shiel on the A87. There is roadside parking nearby for about a dozen cars. Either car shuffle or lock a bike at the Cluanie Inn (at the western end of Loch

LEFT SIGNPOST AT THE START   **ABOVE** SKIRTING SGÙRR BEAG

from Sgùrr an Doire Leathain is awesome. If there are people on it, they look like ants from your viewpoint on the summit. Really take it in! This section is a bit longer. After descending to a bealach, keep right to skirt the small top immediately ahead. You now reach a flat section and bend to the right slightly to finally ascend Maol Chinn-dearg.

❻ There is a cracking view from here towards the highest summit – Aonach air Chrith, but it is quite a hard climb up to the top! Descend Maol Chinn-dearg and follow the ridge to begin the long climb on to Aonach air Chrith.

❼ This final section is a bit of a slog. Drop off Aonach air Chrith into a bealach, which curves slightly to the left. You will come to a fork in the path; keep right to avoid a pointless climb to a nondescript summit, which is properly tough on tired legs (trust me: I did this for you, dear reader). Once you've scrambled over the rocky top of Druim Shionnach you can see the final top of Creag a' Mhàim ahead. Descend into the bealach on a wonderful section of the ridge before a final climb to the top.

❽ Once you are on Creag a' Mhàim, descend south-east and join the zigzag path down the hill. At the bottom, turn left and join the big track. This is actually an old military road, part of which is now submerged by nearby Loch Loyne, following its enlargement when a hydroelectric dam was constructed in the 1950s. You can refill your water bottle at the nearby river, if needed. Once you have steeled yourself for a long run home, start heading north on the track that is initially uphill. You then have a largely downhill 5km run to the Cluanie Inn, where they may well be a hearty meal and a beer awaiting you. The river close to the end is also very nice for a dip on a warm day.

Cluanie) for a (mostly) downhill pedal at the end.

There are no practical public transport options for this route.

TOP TIP
Make sure to take enough water with you – it can be tricky to find water on ridges. On this route there is plenty of water on the way up and at the end.

OTHER OPTIONS
There are a couple of opportunities to drop off the ridge earlier if you do not feel up to the full 27 kilometres. The main shortened route is off Maol Chinn-dearg. When on the summit, head north-east off the ridge, following a protruding shoulder (or spur). This connects to a zigzag path that leads to a car park on the A87 approximately 8 kilometres east of the start of the route (16km; 1,435m ascent).

WHERE TO REFUEL
The Cluanie Inn has long been a favourite haunt of those exploring Kintail. Drop in for a hot meal or, if baking and coffee is more your fancy, they have recently opened the **Landour Bakehouse** directly opposite.

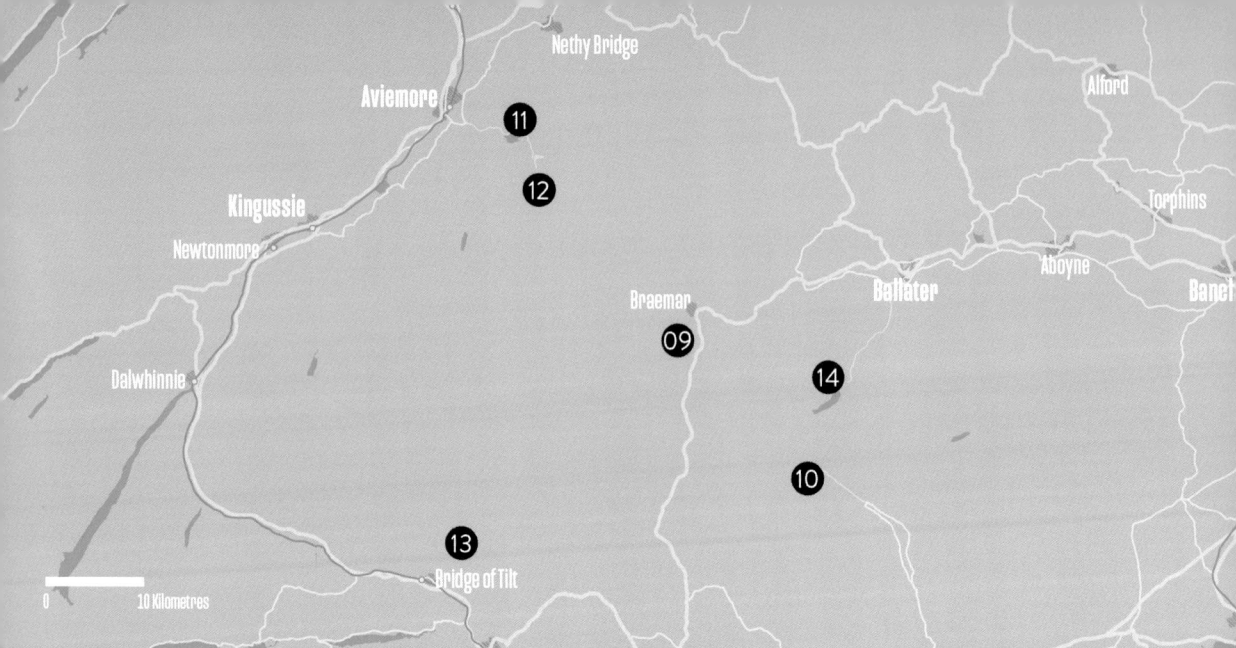

Scottish writer Nan Shepherd managed to forge an entire literary career from the Cairngorms, and she encapsulated their magic in her book *The Living Mountain*.

The Cairngorms National Park is the UK's largest – and it is a paradise for the trail or hill runner.

The Cairngorms themselves are a grand granite plateau, eroded and scarred from thousands of years of ice ages, which cut deep glens like the Lairig Ghru through this awe-inspiring massif.

The rounded tops and deep glens make for astonishingly good running (and skiing), with the granite providing a reliable surface for trail runners. At their feet, the Cairngorms are home to the remnant Caledonian pine forest – a habitat native to Scotland, providing a home to a range of special creatures like capercaillie, pine marten, red squirrels, osprey and black grouse. This habitat is a shadow of its former self, but it is starting to make a comeback.

Thanks to its arctic–alpine conditions, the range is also home to the longest-surviving snow patch in the UK – the Sphinx, which sits at the foot of Braeriach. The cold climate makes for some astonishing arctic plants too, as well as some testing conditions.

You could write a whole book about the running to be had in this vast place. It is also steeped in hill-running history, with several iconic routes tracing their way across the plateau: the Rigby Round, the Big 6, the Cairngorm 4000s and, more recently, it is the place most runners go to run as many Munros as they can in under 24 hours.

The routes in this section take in a large part of the national park: south to Beinn a' Ghlo, east to Angus and several in the heart of the Cairngorms themselves.

OPPOSITE *LOCHNAGAR RIDGE* (ROUTE 14)

CAIRNGORMS

'Standing at the heart of the brilliant universe of the Cairngorms, Morrone is the mountain every hill runner wishes they could escape so easily to from their village, town or city.' JONNY MUIR

Jonny is a teacher, hill runner and author whose book, *The Mountains are Calling*, explores the 'beautiful madness' of hill running in Scotland. He lives in Edinburgh and is a member of Carnethy Hill Running Club.

09
MORRONE
11km

Here we are – back where it all began. The sport of hill running – as much as we can tell – was a trial to find the fastest runners to operate a postal service across the wild and unforgiving lands of the Scottish Highlands.

According to Jonny Muir in his book *The Mountains are Calling*, the Braemar Gathering was established under the decree of King Malcolm III, and it was under his rule in the eleventh century that the first Braemar hill races were run. Back then, the testing ground was the diminutive yet brutal peak of Creag Choinnich. In fact, it was so brutal that Queen Victoria, in 1850, banned hill running after one of her gamekeepers was never quite himself again after winning the race. Mercifully, Queen Elizabeth II reinstated the hill race at the Braemar Gathering in 1979, and around 100 runners every year dash up the new venue, Morrone, on the other side of the A93.

While a straightforward route, Morrone provides an excellent, easy day out with high bang-for-your-buck points. The gradual slope allows time for you to enjoy the sensational views, while the descent provides for some exciting running on good ground.

I find Morrone to be a far better run than hike, as the easy gradient drags on when walking but is much more fun running. This is a great hill if you've spent a few days running in the big hills and need a break, or you're on your way up or down the A93.

With an obvious path throughout, not much in the way of difficult ground and cracking views, you will enjoy this one!

Distance 11km   **Ascent** 605m   **Time** 2–3 hours   **Start** Braemar   **Start latitude/longitude** 57.0031, -3.4125
Start grid reference NO 143911   **Difficulty** 1/5 – Easy running on good paths, with some rocky parts   **Bogs** 1/5 – No bogs!   **Terrain** Paths, trails and some rocky parts up high   **Map** Harvey Ultramap, Cairn Gorm & Ben Avon (1:40,000)

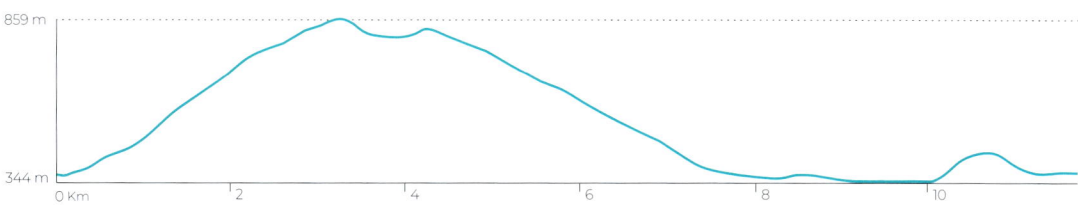

OPPOSITE *DESCENT TO THE ROAD*

BRAEMAR DUCK POND

ABOVE *VIEW OVER BRAEMAR* BELOW *THE FINAL CLIMB*

DIRECTIONS

S From the car park, follow the path that exits from the corner by the duck pond. Follow the path to a small woodland and a deer fence, after which the path joins a large track. Head up to the left, as it climbs a little. Ignore the signpost with an arrow pointing right; instead, go straight up into the woods again and pop out at a lovely clearing with a bench and a viewpoint marker. Take a moment to peruse this and maybe even enjoy a view over the hills which it indicates. Continue through the bushes and join a path. Continue straight across to the trees. Ignore the sign pointing right for *Morrone Birkwood*; instead follow the one that simply says *Morrone*. However, it's worth noting that Morrone Birkwood, a Special Area of Conservation, is a unique natural environment, with the same flora having been present since the end of the last ice age.

2 The ascent now begins gradually. Leave the trees behind again and slowly make your way up the hill, providing ever more impressive views over

ABOVE *FINAL DESCENT TOWARDS THE ROAD*
BELOW *THE DESCENT*   RIGHT *VIEWFINDER AT THE FOOT OF MORRONE OVERLOOKING THE CAIRNGORM PLATEAU*

the Cairngorms beyond. It steepens for a short while, but levels out again. At about two-thirds of the way up, you will see the Five Cairns. This is the point where the hill race turns around back to the games field.

❸ Carry on uphill for another 1km on a wide, rocky path to reach the summit of Morrone. The giant mast somewhat mars the otherwise incredible surroundings: look north over the Cairngorms, east to Lochnagar and south over Glen Shee. Below, you have a cool bird's-eye view over Braemar. It really is a great bang-for-your buck run, as you've only ran 3.3km so far!

❹ Continue over the summit, passing the radio mast and buildings, over initially rocky ground before hitting a very clear vehicle track. This winds its way south-east and then east, eventually popping out on the Old Military Road.

❺ Turn left and jog along the road for 2.4km, leaving the tarmac briefly to detour on a path through Balintuim. Pass through the golf course and, as you pass the clubhouse, turn left to follow a blue waymarker. Head up the hill, past some caravans and through a gate into a lovely woodland. Continue heading uphill for a short stint before popping out next to a cattle grid. Follow the track and you will find yourself back at the signpost you saw at the start. Turn right and retrace your steps back to the start.

POINTS OF INTEREST
- **Corbett** Morrone, 859m

HIGHLIGHTS
- Clear path
- Runnable trails
- Excellent views
- Lovely woodland to finish

GETTING THERE
A direct bus runs from Aberdeen to Braemar; it takes a long time to get all the way from Aberdeen, but this may be a good option if you're staying east of Braemar. If arriving by car, there is a free car park at the start of the route (the car park has a 2m height restriction). Alternatively, there are some lay-bys on a minor road just north of the start of the route (grid reference: NO 144914).

TOP TIP
Fancy a challenge? The Braemar Gathering has a race on Morrone in early September to the Five Cairns and back. Have a crack at this race which has an excellent history.

OTHER OPTIONS
You can, of course, make the route an out-and-back to the summit of Morrone (7km; 483m ascent).

If you have been smashing the big hills for days and need a very low-level run, follow the Birkwood circular path at the foot of Morrone. The loop is around 4.5 kilometres long and very flat.

WHERE TO REFUEL
Having spent many a family holiday in Braemar, I can say – without hesitation – you have to visit **The Bothy**. They have it all: brilliant breakfast, cakes, sandwiches and coffee. If it's a later meal you are after, the **Hungry Highlander** chippy (opposite The Bothy) is ideal, or **The Cairn** restaurant.

'Exiting the trees, I am always amazed by the rugged beauty of Corrie Fee. There's a well-placed rock where I like to sit and soak in the atmosphere and – if I am lucky – be joined by a squirrel or see an eagle. There's no better place to be.' RICHARD BANNISTER

Richard is a Deeside-based runner who loves running in the mountains with a particular focus on skyrunning, especially the UK races in the Lake District.

10
MAYAR, DRIESH AND CORRIE FEE
15km

Nestled in a remote corner of Scotland, right at the edge of the Cairngorms National Park, is a truly magical place. The two peaks of Mayar and Driesh can be overlooked due to their pudding-like tops, but these two hills make for some excellent trail running, with forest tracks in the glen and runnable terrain between the summits.

The highlight, though, is Corrie Fee. Like a massive rocky armchair, this glacial corrie emerges before you between the pine trees – a natural amphitheatre tucked away in an isolated corner of Scotland.

The corrie forms part of the Corrie Fee National Nature Reserve and features rare arctic–alpine plants and Scotland's largest area of montane willow scrub, which is an excellent habitat for ground-nesting birds. Look out for eagles, peregrine falcons, red deer and (possibly) pine martens while you are in the area.

The route follows forest tracks into Corrie Fee and ascends its steep back on to the summit of Mayar. On a clear day, I often feel you can look out and see the whole of Scotland from there. It's then an easy trot to Driesh on runnable ground followed by a fun descent back to the start of the route.

Distance 15km **Ascent** 816m **Time** 2–3 hours **Start** Glen Doll **Start latitude/longitude** 56.8708, -3.1762 **Start grid reference** NO 284761 **Difficulty** 1/5 – Rolling terrain and good trails **Bogs** 2/5 – Mostly dry but some parts along tops could be boggy after rain **Terrain** Forest trails at start and end; grassier on the tops **Map** Harvey Superwalker, Lochnagar & Glen Shee (1:25,000)

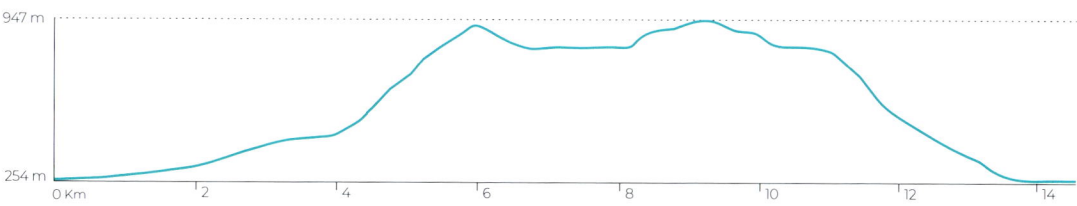

OPPOSITE *TOP OF CORRIE FEE*

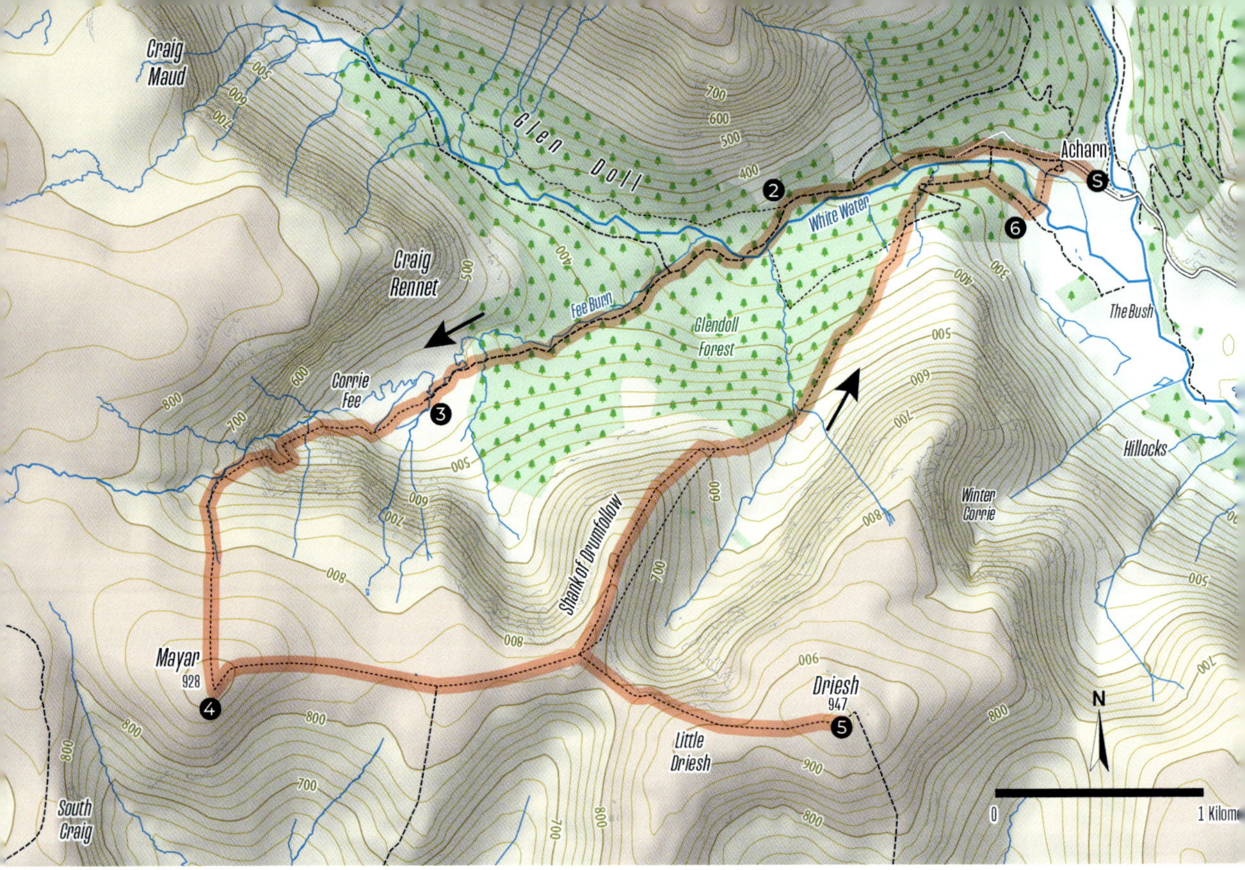
Craig Maud
Glen Doll
Acharn
S
2
White Water
6
The Bush
Fee Burn
Glendoll Forest
Craig Rennet
Corrie Fee
3
Hillocks
Winter Corrie
Shank of Drumfollow
Mayar
928
4
Driesh
947
5
Little Driesh
South Craig
N
0
1 Kilom

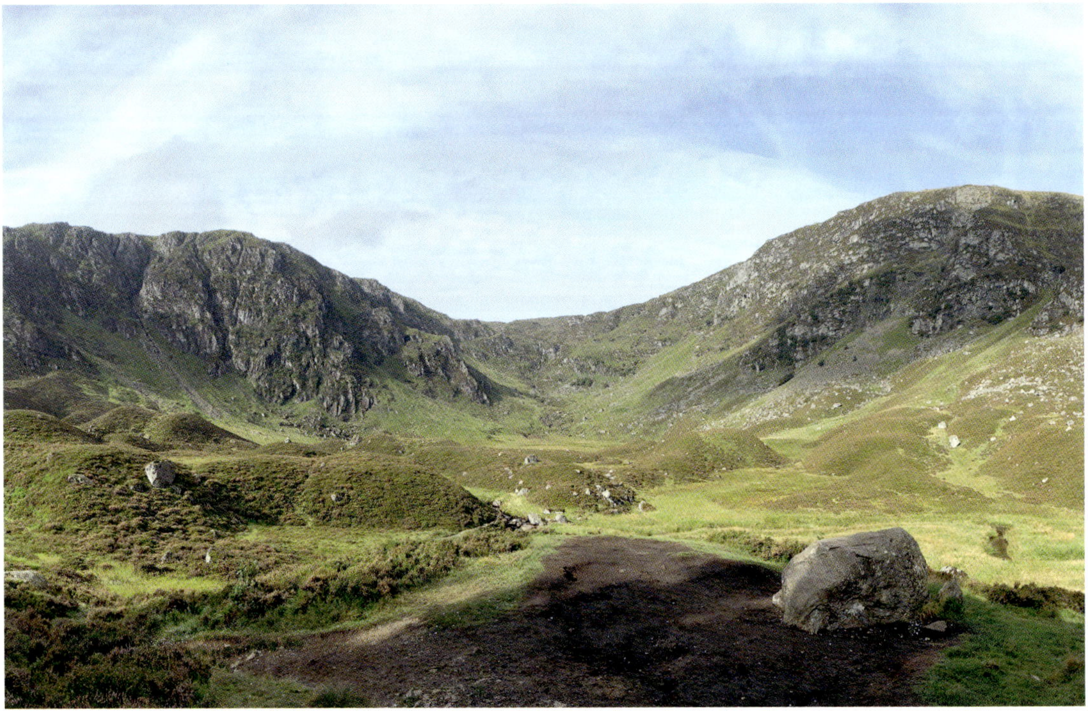

CORRIE FEE

ABOVE *VIEW FROM THE START* BELOW *CORRIE FEE SIGN*

DIRECTIONS

S From the car park, take the track to the left of the visitor centre where a sign marks *Forest Trails*. Bear left at a fork and continue into the pine forest, ignoring any tracks breaking off to the right. You're now on Jock's Road, an old drove road which was used to drive cattle between Angus in the east and Braemar over the hills. Interestingly, in the nineteenth century the estate banned people walking the path. John (Jock) Winter, a local shepherd, defied it and, backed by the Scottish Rights of Way Society, won a lawsuit against the estate. Scotland's very own Kinder Trespass!

2 Fork left, leaving Jock's Road, then cross the river and fork right, following the green markers. The track now climbs steadily and turns into a walkers' path into the trees. All of a sudden, the pines peel apart to reveal the magical Corrie Fee beyond. Take the time to soak this in – it really is a wonderful place.

VIEW TOWARDS GLEN DOLL

3 Run into the corrie, following the babbling river up towards the back wall of the corrie. The path now steepens, skirting below a curtain-like waterfall. After a short climb, the path levels out and bends to the left up an easier climb to the summit of Mayar, your first Munro.

4 From the summit you can see right across the Cairngorm Plateau and north to Lochnagar and its neighbouring peaks. To the east, about 3km away, you can see the top of Driesh. Turn left at the summit and begin to follow a long line of old metal fenceposts. After around 2km, drop down to the right on a path and head up Little Driesh. This is a just a wee climb, followed by a gentle gradient up to the second Munro, (Big) Driesh.

5 Retrace your steps back over Little Driesh and down into the bealach. From there, bear right and take the descent path down the side of the hill. Follow this great path down to the forestry plantation, across a river and descend to meet the forest tracks below. Cross the first track on to another path and join the track lower down. Remember, plantations are commercial forests and often have machinery moving around, so bear that in mind and remember the tracks may change slightly over time.

6 Cross a bridge and re-emerge on to your outward route. Turn right at this junction and follow the track to the car park.

ABOVE WATERFALL ON THE ROUTE
BELOW WOODLAND ON THE ROUTE

POINTS OF INTEREST
- Corrie Fee
- **Munro** Mayar, 928m
- **Munro** Driesh (Thornbush), 947m

HIGHLIGHTS
- The incredible Corrie Fee
- Excellent running along the tops
- Great trails in the glen
- Superb views across the Cairngorms

GETTING THERE
There are no practical public transport options for this route.

The journey to the start at Glen Doll can feel like an adventure in itself – it is quite remote, and driving is really the only way to get there. There is a pay-and-display car park with toilets and a visitor centre at the start of the route.

TOP TIP
Phone signal is non-existent on the route, unless you're right on the tops. Download any maps or GPX files you need before you go.

OTHER OPTIONS
For an alternative descent off Driesh take a bearing slightly east of north from the summit and descend by the Scorrie Ridge. It is a nice, grassy ridge back down into the forest, with occasional steep sections.

You can cut the route short by missing out the spur to Driesh – follow the route until the bealach before Little Driesh and descend back into the forest (12km; 696m ascent). Another option is to follow Jock's Road into Glen Doll, turning right after 7km. The path eventually follows the River South Esk back to the car park (16km; 600m ascent).

Of course, there are a number of marked trails in the forest providing some pleasant shorter options.

WHERE TO REFUEL
You will have to travel a bit to grab a bite to eat, but on your way you could stop at the **Drovers Inn**, a traditional Scottish pub in Memus. For great coffee, tasty toasties and other goodies, I would check out **88°** in Kirriemuir.

LOVED THIS ROUTE?
To learn more about Corrie Fee National Nature Reserve and its natural significance, head to **www.nature.scot**

'The Meall a' Bhuachaille ridge has satisfying quantities of everything – rocks, heather and bog – and is often an island of good weather when the bigger hills surrounding it are smothered in cloud.' ALLY BEAVEN

Ally is a part-time barman and the author of the seminal work on dot-watching: *Broken* (published by Vertebrate Publishing). He's also not too shabby at running – he holds the bad weather course record at the An Teallach Hill Race and he recently broke his streak of not finishing Big Rounds by completing Ramsay's Round in 2021.

11
MEALL A' BHUACHAILLE *16km*

While the Cairngorm Plateau stands mightily above Loch Morlich, feeling all pompous about how good it looks, the small but mighty Meall a' Bhuachaille stands on its northern shore – and it too should feel pompous!

Meall a' Bhuachaille (otherwise known as Ally Beaven's favourite hill) is a belter of a hill. It cannot boast Munro status, but its ridge and surrounding Caledonian pine forest are an absolute treat.

On a sunny day, you'd be forgiven for thinking you were running through somewhere like Oregon, so sublime are the trails and wild the woods. Not far from Aviemore and the A9, Meall a' Bhuachaille makes for an easily accessible route too.

Starting out on easy trails, you will pass the famous An Lochan Uaine – the Green Lochan. Local legend says that the loch is green because fairies (little tricksters and pests in Scottish folklore) wash their clothes in it. The truth is likely to do with the reflections of the pine trees and some algae (though, there are stories of leeches). You will also pass the popular Ryvoan Bothy and look across to the rejuvenating deciduous woodland of Abernethy Forest that is being nursed back to health by the RSPB.

Once on the ridge, you will enjoy phenomenal views down into the Ryvoan Pass and up to the Cairngorms. Bobbing all the way to Craiggowrie, you will have to drop down a pretty muddy path back to the forest, but that's all part of the fun!

Keep your eye out for eagles, ospreys, hares and – if you're super lucky – a rare capercaillie. You can also stop at the reindeer centre and see something a bit different. The Caledonian pine forest is an incredible ecosystem, so take the time to enjoy these ancient forests.

Distance 16km   **Ascent** 757m   **Time** 2–4 hours   **Start** Glenmore   **Start latitude/longitude** 57.1667, -3.6916   **Start grid reference** NH 978097   **Difficulty** 2/5 – Nothing technical except a tricky descent early on and a rough bog on the final descent   **Bogs** 3/5 – Mostly dry on ridge with some wet patches, but can be quite boggy on the final descent   **Terrain** Mostly good trails but with some wet ground on the ridge   **Map** OS Explorer OL57, Cairn Gorm & Aviemore (1:25,000)

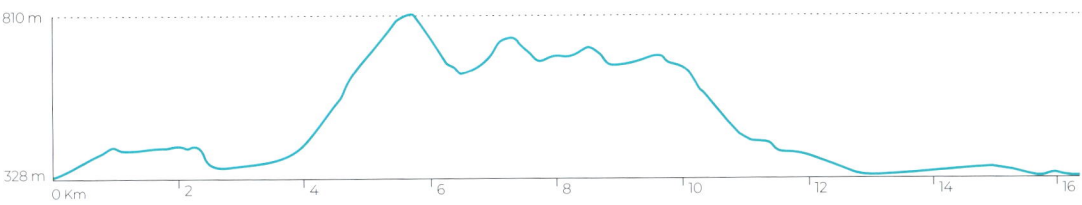

OPPOSITE *THE CLIMB TO RYVOAN BOTHY*

DIRECTIONS

S Follow the road uphill from Glenmore, to the left of the Cairngorm Reindeer Centre; there is a little blue waymarker here, which is part of the Ryvoan Trail. Keep right as you pass a house on the corner and head up the long, open gravel track. The views get steadily more impressive as you climb. The path enters the forest and, when you pop out of the forest again, you get a grand view towards the Ryvoan Pass ahead and the Cairngorms on your right. Drop into the woods again on a steep and rooty path, which is slightly technical. Once you're out of the woods again, it is a short jog over some boardwalks before you come to the amazing An Lochan Uaine.

2 Once you have grabbed some snaps, take the left fork and head towards Ryvoan Bothy. At the bothy, turn left and begin the long climb up Meall a' Bhuachaille. It goes without saying that the views here are amazing – probably the best of the whole route. The views down to the lochan are quite dramatic and, if the Cairngorms have snow, they look so impressive. Behind you and to the right is Abernethy Forest – one of the largest areas of native forest in the UK. Hopefully the views will be impressive enough to distract you from the arduous climb. It's straightforward and has steps to help but is quite steep. Eventually, the large cairn atop Meall a' Bhuachaille comes into view.

3 Drop off the summit on a winding path down to the bealach and a path junction. The main path now heads down to the left, but our route goes straight ahead on to a smaller trail. Descend a little, hop a bog and then follow the path up Creagan Gorm.

4 You will see the ridge stretch out ahead of you (hopefully). Leave Creagan Gorm heading north-west and follow the undulating ridge. The path does go through some boggy patches here and there, all of which are fine if it has been dry but could require a bit more bog hopping in rainier seasons.

RUNNING ADVENTURES SCOTLAND

ABOVE *A BOARDWALK EARLY ON IN THE ROUTE*
RIGHT *PATH THROUGH THE TREES* **BELOW** *FOREST TRAIL*

11 MEALL A' BHUACHAILLE

TOP LEFT *AN LOCHAN UAINE* **LEFT** *ENTERING THE RYVOAN PASS* **ABOVE** *MEALL A' BHUACHAILLE SUMMIT* **BELOW** *BOGGY DESCENT FROM CRAIGGOWRIE*

MEALL A' BHUACHAILLE DESCENT

POINTS OF INTEREST
- An Lochan Uaine (Green Lochan)
- Ryvoan Bothy
- **Corbett** Meall a' Bhuachaille, 810m
- **Summit** Creagan Gorm, 732m
- **Summit** Craiggowrie, 687m

HIGHLIGHTS
- Beautiful woodlands
- Great trails
- Epic views over the Cairngorms
- A dip in Loch Morlich at the end

GETTING THERE
Trains run between Perth and Inverness, stopping at Aviemore. Buses run between Aviemore and Glenmore. Alternatively, there is a pay-and-display car park at Glenmore Visitor Centre.

TOP TIP
Enjoyed this route? How about giving the race a try! Usually held in October, the Meall a' Bhuachaille hill race is a lot of fun.

OTHER OPTIONS
To shorten the route, follow the main route until you reach the path junction in the bealach between Meall a' Bhuachaille and Creagan Gorm. Turn left here, heading down some steps towards the treeline. Some orange waymarkers lead you down through the pines and on to a track. You can then follow signs for *Glenmore Visitor Centre* (9km; 551m ascent).

WHERE TO REFUEL
At the foot of Meall a' Bhuachaille is the famous **Pine Marten Bar**, serving good beer and decent grub in a fantastic location. **Glenmore Visitor Centre** also serves food. Aviemore has a few great places to grab a bite to eat. At the time of writing, a new pizza place has opened above the Cairngorm Mountain Sports shop: **Cheese and Tomatin**. There's also **Coffee Corner** next to Nevisport and the cafe inside **Tiso** is really good too.

LOVED THIS ROUTE?
The Glenmore area is hugely important for wildlife; learn more at the visitor centre. Meall a' Bhuachaille is part of the Abernethy National Nature Reserve. Learn more at **www.nature.scot/abernethy**

5 Craiggowrie is always just one top further than you think. Eventually, you reach its rocky top and can enjoy the magical views over Strathspey. Continue over the summit and drop down a small rocky section on to the path. The path now slowly bends left and descends south-west. Pass a large cairn, where the path is still good. After a short distance, though, the ground becomes wetter and muddier. In places a path resides, but much of the descent is a little muddy. It isn't too technical – actually, we found it quite fun, and it is especially fun in the Meall a' Bhuachaille hill race when you have to run as fast as you can down here!

6 As the descent bottoms out, there is a bit of a swamp to get through, that is passable by some skilled bog hopping on to tufts of grass and stones. Aim for the forest where the path dries up and drops down over some roots on to a forestry track. Now there is a long, fast descent on the gravel path down to the Badaguish Outdoor Centre.

7 Stick to the road through the centre. Just before you leave, take a gravel path on the left and go through a green swing gate. Follow the open forestry track for 200m before keeping right at a fork. Continue along the track as it descends to the road. Follow the path next to the road and, where you come to the youth hostel, keep left to go around it. Soon you will be back at the start of the route, ready for a swim in Loch Morlich.

'The Cairngorms are such a rich and unique landscape, not just within the UK but compared with a lot of the places I have run in. It is a landscape that keeps giving: the more you explore it and learn its idiosyncrasies, the more you come to appreciate it.' GEORGIA TINDLEY

Georgia is a Highlands-based skyrunner. If she isn't running up and down the hills, she'll have her nose in a book or be riding her bike around her beloved Isle of Lewis.

12
CAIRNGORM PLATEAU
20km

The Cairngorms National Park is the biggest of the UK's 15 national parks. The mountains that lie within it have inspired many, but perhaps the most keenly of them is Nan Shepherd.

Shepherd wrote the now-semi-famous natural adventure book, *The Living Mountain*. Despite its slim spine, *The Living Mountain* is full of a lifetime of Shepherd's experiences in the Cairngorms. Her poetry is also a love letter to the mountains that inspired her to write fiction and non-fiction about the people and nature that surround them.

The route I have for you takes inspiration from Shepherd, taking you on to the high plateau, past Loch A'an and Loch Etchachan, near the small lochans in Coire an Lochain (all great for a dip), and over Scotland's second- and sixth-highest peaks: Ben Macdui and Cairn Gorm. All of it is very runnable.

Not only is the plateau a place of literary inspiration, but it is also a magnificent space for nature. Parallels are often drawn between here and the Hardangervidda plateau in Norway. They share many characteristics and the Hardangervidda shows how Scotland's plateau could look with some restoration.

You will very likely come across ptarmigans on the plateau, along with eagles, deer and maybe even the reindeer from the local reindeer centre.

Distance 20km   **Ascent** 1,245m   **Time** 3–5 hours   **Start** Cairngorm Mountain ski centre   **Start latitude/longitude** 57.1338, -3.6703   **Start grid reference** NH 990060   **Difficulty** 2/5 – Minor scrambling down to Loch A'an but largely easy running   **Bogs** 1/5 – This is the dry section of the Cairngorms!   **Terrain** Almost entirely paths and trails with some boulder sections   **Map** Harvey Ultramap, Cairn Gorm & Ben Avon (1:40,000).

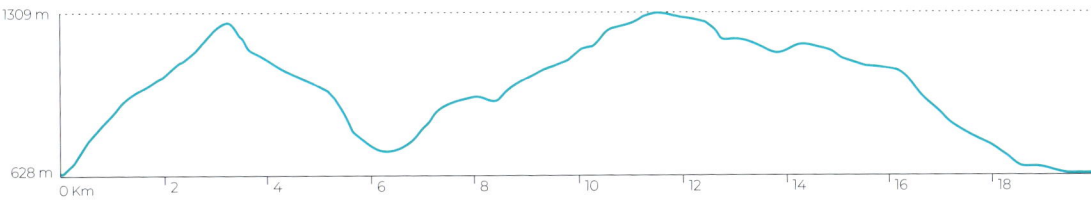

OPPOSITE *OVERLOOKING LOCH ETCHACHAN FROM BEINN MHEADHOIN*

LOCH A'AN

DIRECTIONS

S From the ski centre, climb up the Windy Ridge Path. This is accessed on the left-hand side of the car park as you enter it, with signposts indicating the way. Climb for 2.5km, coming to the Ptarmigan Station. A cobbled path now heads uphill, taking you to the summit of Cairn Gorm at 1,244m, Scotland's sixth-highest mountain.

2 From the summit mast, bear right on a faint path down on to the plateau where you come to a junction. Turn left to head south-east on a great trail that descends – first gradually but eventually steeply – down to Loch A'an. Take care on the steep section; it isn't technical, just a bit loose in places.

3 If it's a nice day, take a dip (or a dook, as we say in Scotland) in the loch. Also, look out for the shelter stone as you make your way around the western shore. There are a few quite similar to it, which are basically large boulders that allow for walkers to bivouac under them to escape the weather. Follow the path on the western side of Loch A'an under the cliffs of Càrn Etchachan and climb up the path heading south to follow the river. At the top, you reach Loch Etchachan, one of Shepherd's favourite places for a dip.

4 Run up the clear path to a junction, taking the right-hand path to climb gradually along a hillside. Heading south-west, you will soon follow the river that feeds Loch Etchachan.

ABOVE *LOOKING DOWN CAIRN GORM TOWARDS THE NORTHERN CORRIES* **BELOW** *DESCENDING BEN MACDUI* **OPPOSITE PAGE** *LOCH A'AN*

The trail slowly bends right up a steeper section, with a final long drag up Ben Macdui. The summit is just beyond an old shelter known as the Sapper's Bothy, which was used by Ordnance Survey to house its surveyors as they mapped the UK in the nineteenth century.

❺ Bear right off the summit, gradually descending until the ground flattens out. Bear left at a fork and head north along a plateau. Skirt round the hillside and, around 4km after you left the summit of Ben Macdui, you will come to the descent off the Northern Corries.

❻ The Northern Corries are truly spectacular and very popular with climbers, particularly Coire an t-Sneachda. There are routes you can take that skirt along their edge, with some great scrambling in places. The lochans in the corries are also nice, quiet places for a swim. For now, drop down on an initially steep path that becomes very runnable, slowly bending to the right and taking you all the way back to the ski centre.

POINTS OF INTEREST
- **Munro** Cairn Gorm (Blue Mountain), 1,244m
- **Munro** Ben Macdui (MacDuff's Hill), 1,309m
- Loch A'an
- Loch Etchachan

HIGHLIGHTS
- Easy running across the plateau
- Taste of Nordic wilderness
- Views from each of the Munros
- The final descent

GETTING THERE
Trains run between Perth and Inverness, stopping at Aviemore; buses run between Aviemore and the Cairngorm Mountain ski centre.

Alternatively, the Coire Cas car park is the main ski car park at the foot of the Cairn Gorm mountain. It's a very popular spot for walkers, but with ample space for parking. There is a £2 donation requested for parking there.

TOP TIP
If the weather is good, take the time to go for a swim along the route: Loch A'an, Loch Etchachan and the small lochans in Coire an Lochain are great. Otherwise, Loch Morlich, which is located to the north of our route, is also an ace spot – it even has a beach!

OTHER OPTIONS
There are lots of ways to extend or change this route up a bit. To run along the edge of the Northern Corries follow the main route to the summit of Cairn Gorm and down to the junction mentioned at the start of **2**. Instead of turning left, go straight ahead, heading south-west, and run along the rim of the corries. Descend via the route mentioned in **6** (11km; 782m ascent).

To add some mileage to the route you can add Beinn Mheadhoin to your list of Munros by following the main route until the Loch Etchachan junction in **4**. Turn left here and follow the zigzag path to the lunar-like summit of Beinn Mheadhoin. Retrace your steps to the Loch Etchachan junction then continue on the main route (23km; 1,495m ascent).

Additionally, you can descend Ben Macdui via its southern route into the Lairig Ghru. From there you can return via this trail (33km; 2,014m ascent), or you can make a monster day out and go up the Munros in the west – the Devil's Point, Cairn Toul, Sgòr an Lochain Uaine and Braeriach (43km; 2,950m ascent).

WHERE TO REFUEL
By Loch Morlich, there is the famous **Pine Marten Bar**, which serves good beer and decent grub in a fantastic location. **Glenmore Visitor Centre** also serves food. Aviemore has a few great places to grab a bite to eat. At the time of writing, a new pizza place has opened above the Cairngorm Mountain Sports shop: **Cheese and Tomatin**. There's also **Coffee Corner** next to Nevisport and the cafe inside **Tiso** is really good too.

LOVED THIS ROUTE?
Learn more about the great conservation work going on in the Cairngorms National Park at **www.cairngorms.co.uk**, where you'll find details of current projects and ways to get involved.

'Beinn a' Ghlo is a mountain of adventure for me, having seemingly visited every gully and rocky knoll on my first Lowe Alpine Mountain Marathon, and crossed its summits – at the end of a two-day-long epic – on my Munro Round. It's a complex range, full of surprises and far-reaching views from its high, sweeping ridges to the wilderness beyond.' STEPHEN PYKE

Stephen (aka Spyke) is a member of Dark Peak Fell Runners and lives in the Eastern Lake District. He loves big adventures in the hills, especially Scotland, and has held records for the Munro Round, Tranter's Round and the Scottish 4000s.

13
BEINN A' GHLO
22km

On a map, Beinn a' Ghlo is an absolute mess of contour lines: they tangle themselves around the various corries that scour the massif. It's like Beinn a' Ghlo was once a great castle fired at by canons which blasted out these big holes in its sides.

Beinn a' Ghlo (Hill of the Mist) stands as one of the most southerly ranges of the Cairngorm mountains, right at the gateway to the Highlands on the A9. The area around this group of three Munros is known as Highland Perthshire, which is one of the most stunning parts of Scotland – particularly in autumn, where its immense number of trees turn the whole area golden.

Given Beinn a' Ghlo's rocky qualities, it is unsurprising that this area has been of interest to geologists for some time. The 'father of geology', James Hutton, made discoveries in nearby Glen Tilt that helped him realise that granite was formed by the cooling of molten rock. It also helped in theorising that the geological timeline was long – like, *really* long.

I adore this route. The ridge winds its way between three beautiful peaks, and any time you look back where you came you marvel at just the scale of them. It's easy to feel like you are a tiny person running along a huge dragon's back. Easily accessed from the A9, this makes for an excellent run en route to the Highlands or as part of an exploration of Highland Perthshire.

Beinn a' Ghlo is also a Site of Special Scientific Interest and Special Area of Conservation due to its rare alpine flora; stick to the main paths to avoid squashing these delicate plants.

Distance 22km **Ascent** 1,226m **Time** 3–5 hours **Start** Loch Moraig **Start latitude/longitude** 56.7826, -3.7921 **Start grid reference** NN 906671 **Difficulty** 2/5 – Occasional rough ground with first climb quite steep, but otherwise undulating ridges **Bogs** 2/5 – Bottom of first climb and final descent often boggy, but ridge is usually dry **Terrain** Rocky with paths **Map** Harvey Superwalker, Pitlochry, Loch Tummel & Blair Atholl (1:25,000)

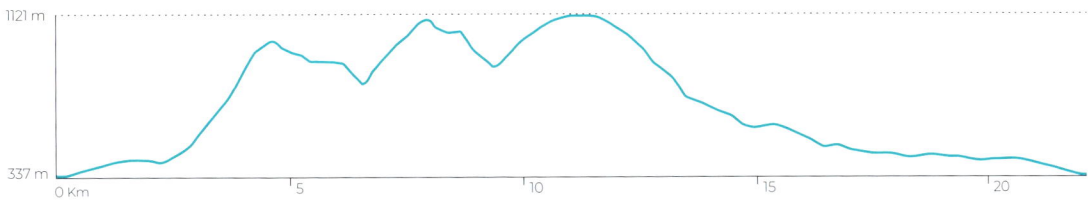

OPPOSITE *RUNNING FROM CARN LIATH*

LOOKING SOUTH TOWARDS CARN LIATH © PAUL WEBSTER

DIRECTIONS

S As you step out your car (or off your bike – if so, chapeau), you will notice you are quite high up. Follow the road a short way (heading north-east) and take the right-hand track at the end of the cluster of trees. Climb on this 4x4 track and go through a gate to where the track flattens out.

2 Turn left, leaving the track and following a faint path past a small hut. Beyond this hut, the path follows a series of grouse butts towards the base of the hill. This part can be quite wet underfoot, but it is one of the few boggy sections of the day. Soon, you are heading up the unforgivingly steep slope of Carn Liath. The path has been a key focus for repair works over the years, with the erosion scar now visible from nearly 50 kilometres away. The ground is loose underfoot which makes it even more challenging at times, and it is easy to see why people are tempted to avoid the main path. Hopefully, by the time you read this, a lot of work will have been done to repair the path. At 900m elevation, the path mercifully levels out, with an easy final trot over rocky ground to the top of Carn Liath. You can almost see the start of the route from the top.

3 The going from here is relatively straightforward, even if Beinn a' Ghlo is living up to its name as 'Hill of the Mist'. Basically, if you are descending

BEINN A' GHLO © PAUL WEBSTER

steeply, you're going the wrong way. Follow the path north from the summit and skirt the top of the big corrie. This is probably my favourite section – the mountains ahead stand like an open book, inviting you to dive in and uncover their secrets. Continue along this spine to Beinn Mhaol.

❹ From Beinn Mhaol, the path dives down into a steep bealach, before instantly shooting back up again on a hard climb on to the next ridge. The view back to Carn Liath is really impressive: the ridgeline snaking down from the summit like a giant letter Z, but a super stylish one made of granite. Your path starts heading north, relenting slightly on a long climb to the summit of Bràigh Coire Chruinn-bhalgain.

❺ Continue from the summit, keeping slightly right and staying above the corries. Now bear left and trot for a couple hundred metres. Before the ground climbs again, head right and straight down the steep slope towards Bealach an Fhiodha. Once in the bealach, you'll see a path following the river on your right – this is your way home later. For now, follow a path that heads uphill and then runs left along the hillside. This is a really excellent section, with some great running all the way to the summit of Carn nan Gabhar. Rather sneakily, the summit isn't actually the trig point – the trig point sits at 1,120m, while the further cairn is at 1,121m.

POINTS OF INTEREST
- **Munro** Carn Liath (Grey Rocky Hill), 975m
- **Munro** Bràigh Coire Chruinn-bhalgain (Upland of the Corrie of Round Lumps), 1,070m
- **Munro** Carn nan Gabhar (Rocky Hill of the Goats), 1,121m

HIGHLIGHTS
- The view north into the Cairngorms
- Amazing ridge off Carn Liath
- Large sections of easy running
- Dramatic corries

GETTING THERE
There is a train station in Blair Atholl, after which it's a 5-kilometre run to the start of the route. Alternatively, there is a large lay-by at the start of the route.

TOP TIP
If you have some time, explore Glen Tilt below. With excellent low-level gravel trails it can make a great day on foot or bike.

OTHER OPTIONS
To shorten the route, after descending Beinn Mhaol turn right on to the path in the bealach between Beinn Mhaol and Bràigh Coire Chruinn-bhalgain (14km; 641m ascent) or do an out-and-back to Bràigh Coire Chruinn-bhalgain (16km; 1,136m ascent).

To take in another side of Beinn a' Ghlo, you could circumnavigate the whole massif on an epic loop (39km; 642m ascent). Glen Tilt is a picturesque and quiet glen to run through, before turning right to pass the creatively-titled Loch Loch and finally turning right to head back to the start.

WHERE TO REFUEL
You are in luck! Blair Atholl, Pitlochry and – if you're heading south – Dunkeld have some *excellent* choices. In Blair Atholl, the **House of Bruar Fish and Chip Shop** is as close as a chippy gets to fine dining. Meanwhile, in Pitlochry, if it's coffee and cake you are after, head to **Cafe Calluna**; for hearty grub, go for **Escape Route**. In Dunkeld, you cannot go wrong with the **Aran Bakery**.

LOVED THIS ROUTE?
The Mend our Mountains campaign is working to reduce the erosion on Carn Liath. Learn more at **www.mountaineering.scot**

6 Retrace your steps back down to the bealach and the aforementioned path by the stream. Follow the boggy path that hugs the river, crossing it a couple of times as the path switches back and forth. Eventually, you stay to the right of the river, on a newly constructed track. This skirts the base of the hillside, eventually descending down to the main 4x4 track.

7 Turn right on to the track, and run in a westerly direction. From here, it's an easy 5km run back along the track to the start of the route.

'The lure of the White Mounth lies with Lochnagar, one of the most recognisable mountains in Scotland. When you're after a long run in the hills it's super easy to add another four Munros to the tick list on very runnable terrain. As a local it's brilliant to have on the doorstep but it's definitely worth the visit if coming from further afield!' HAMISH BATTLE

Hamish has been the Scotland U23 hill running champion and ran in Scotland's hill running team in 2019. He lives in Banchory.

14
WHITE MOUNTH CIRCUIT *29km*

Lochnagar is one of the most majestic mountains in Scotland, in my humble opinion. Its dramatic corrie sits in something of a contrast to the mellow, rolling peaks which hide behind it.

Interestingly, the summit can also be called Cac Carn Beag, which basically translates to mean 'little pile of dung', which is a somewhat less romantic title. Despite its Gaelic name, the mountain is very popular with walkers and climbers alike, but the rest of the White Mounth range is a little less trodden.

The area is just a treat, with a beautiful glen, marvellous loch and excellent trails across the whole range. The views towards the main Cairngorm plateau are amazing, as are those towards the back of the Glen Shee Munros.

For the trail runner looking to run in the hills, this is an excellent trip, without the huge elevation you often find in hill running. The whole route is on good, sandy trails. But don't get too complacent, as the rolling tops can be tricky to find in poor visibility.

Part of the White Mounth range sits in the Balmoral Estate, where the Royal Family hang out when they come to Scotland. Across the whole area, you will see the hallmarks of a bygone era, with old shooting lodges and impressive houses dotted about the vast estate. You'll likely see large herds of red deer in the area and spot the odd ptarmigan.

The route I describe goes anticlockwise, taking the more scenic route up Lochnagar to its impressive crags. It does mean there is a long, flat section along Loch Muick at the end of the route, which can be a drag on tired legs. You are welcome to head the other way and get the long trail out the way first.

Distance 29km **Ascent** 1,175m **Time** 5–7 hours **Start** Spittal of Glenmuick **Start latitude/longitude** 56.9529, -3.1360 **Start grid reference** NO 310852 **Difficulty** 2/5 – Non-technical terrain, but plateau can be difficult to navigate in poor visibility **Bogs** 2/5 – Almost entirely dry, though the middle section can sometimes be wet **Terrain** Excellent paths and trails throughout, with a few grassy trods **Map** Harvey Superwalker, Lochnagar & Glen Shee (1:25,000)

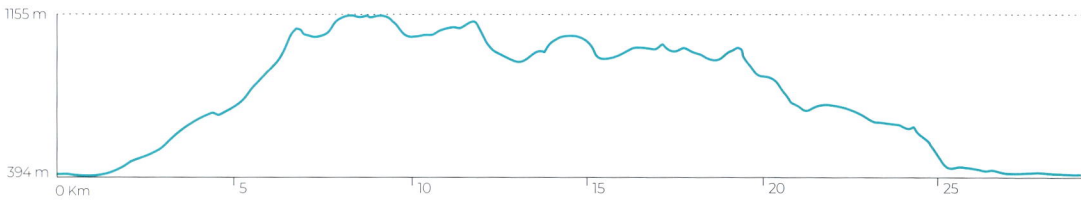

OPPOSITE *SNOW ON THE STUIC CLIFFS*

DIRECTIONS

S Leaving the car park, head across the bridge and past the visitor centre (where they sell flapjacks and soft drinks – woohoo!). Turn right, following the signpost for *Lochnagar* and run along the gravel path to an old shooting lodge. Keep left at the lodge (following another *Lochnagar* signpost next to it) and enter the forest. The path leaves the pines behind and climbs over some rough gravel for 2.5km to reach a large cairn.

2 Turn left at a big cairn and head up the stepped path up towards the bealach. This is quite a nice runnable section – and you're in for a treat at the top!

3 Emerge over the lip of the bealach and be wowed by the sight of Lochnagar's eastern crags, with the loch of the same name below you. It's so 'wow' that Lord Byron wrote a poem about it. Head up a bouldery path on the left, following the edge of the corrie. The path flattens out again, and a line of cairns leads you to the right, slightly downhill before a right-hand turn up another steeper section. You will come across a large cairn, which is named Cac Càrn Mòr. From the glossary of Gaelic terms on page XV, you will know 'mòr' is 'big' and 'beag' is 'small', which should help you to work out the name. Keep going beyond this cairn towards a bigger pile of stones with a trig on the top, marking the summit of Lochnagar Cac Carn Beag. You now have a chance to marvel at the insanely good views out to the Cairngorm plateau to the north, and to Glen Shee in the west.

4 Return to Cac Càrn Mòr and look out for a path that heads to the right. Descend into a shallow bealach with some wet ground in it, before a gradual climb around the next corrie. As it levels out, you will come to a path junction – turn left here and make the short climb to Carn a' Choire Bhoidheach.

5 The path off Carn a' Choire Bhoidheach is quite faint. Head downhill in a westerly direction, following a trod, aiming for the clear path below. I don't think there is 'one' way down, but if you head west and go downhill, you will catch the main path again. Just don't head south from the summit, or you'll be absorbed into the swamp. Trot down the path and cross the Allt an Da Chraobh Bheath, which is a great spot to refill bottles. Skirt around the base of Càrn an t-Sagairt Mòr; when you come to a junction, turn right and head up the hill to the summit.

6 Retrace your steps from the summit of Càrn an t-Sagairt Mòr back to the path junction. Go straight ahead here and pass through a boggy section at the bottom of the next climb. The ascent to Cairn Bannoch is straightforward with a good path, so you can enjoy the views over Glen Shee here. Hopefully you will see the final peak, Broad Cairn, ahead from the summit.

7 Leave Cairn Bannoch but look out for the amazing waterfall on your left as you head along the shoulder of Broad Cairn. Another

TOP LOOKING BACK TO CARN A' CHOIRE BHOIDHEACH **ABOVE** TRACK AFTER THE VISITOR CENTRE **BELOW** SNOW BRIDGE OVER THE ALLT AN DA CHRAOBH BHEATH

gradual climb and a small bouldery section to the summit and you will complete your fifth Munro of the day.

❽ The route off Broad Cairn is initially a bit naff, with lots of boulders and a path which disappears and reappears. If you have good visibility, you should see the red sandy path that descends Broad Cairn not far away, so aim east and watch your ankles as you come off Broad Cairn. Eventually, you reach the good path, and you can zoom down all the way to the little tin hut, which has a bench on the side of it to rest weary legs on.

❾ To avoid spending too long on the track along Loch Muick, ignore the path that heads left soon after the hut, marked by a small cairn, and instead stay high on the wide gravel path. This path undulates slightly for 3km, with some ace views on the left over the first few Munros we passed earlier. Below, you will spot a big house called Glas-allt-Shiel. This was built by Queen Victoria and is now personally owned by Queen Elizabeth II. Behind the house is a bothy, which even has a composting toilet.

❿ Head down the steep zigzag path down to the 4x4 track that runs along Loch Muick. It's now a mostly flat 4km run back to the start where you can grab yourself a cold Irn-Bru from the visitor centre.

ABOVE *LOCHNAGAR CLIFFS* BELOW *HEADING TOWARDS LOCHNAGAR'S SUMMIT*

POINTS OF INTEREST
- **Munro** Lochnagar/Cac Carn Beag, 1,155m
- **Munro** Carn a' Choire Bhoidheach, 1,110m
- **Munro** Càrn an t-Sagairt Mòr, 1,047m
- **Munro** Cairn Bannoch, 1,012m
- **Munro** Broad Cairn, 998m

HIGHLIGHTS
- Superbly runnable trails
- Lochnagar's dramatic face
- Beautiful Loch Muick
- Views over the Cairngorm range
- Bagging five Munros

GETTING THERE
There are no practical public transport options for this route.

The car park at the start of the route is at the Spittal of Glenmuick – head south-west from Ballater to reach it. Parking is becoming a bit trickier but, at the time of writing, there are plans to open an overflow car park. The car park is pay and display.

TOP TIP
The White Mounth is a high plateau, which makes it an exposed place in winter or when it is windy, so be sure to check the mountain weather forecast before heading out.

OTHER OPTIONS
The main way to shorten the route is to take the path from Lochnagar down to Loch Muick. From the summit of Lochnagar, retrace your steps to Cac Càrn Mòr and head south to follow the river down towards Loch Muick.

After descending steeply down the Falls of the Glasallt, which are absolutely stunning, you will pop out at the big house, Glas-allt-Shiel, by Loch Muick. Join the 4x4 track and head east along Loch Muick back to the old shooting lodge. Turn right and you are back at the visitor centre (20km; 864m ascent).

WHERE TO REFUEL
When we ran the White Mounth, we headed back to Ballater to the **Bridge House Cafe**. It has a cute interior and serves brunch *all day*. It also serves waffles, pancakes and some brill soup and paninis.

The Bothy and the **Phoenix Chip Shop** in Ballater are also worth a look.

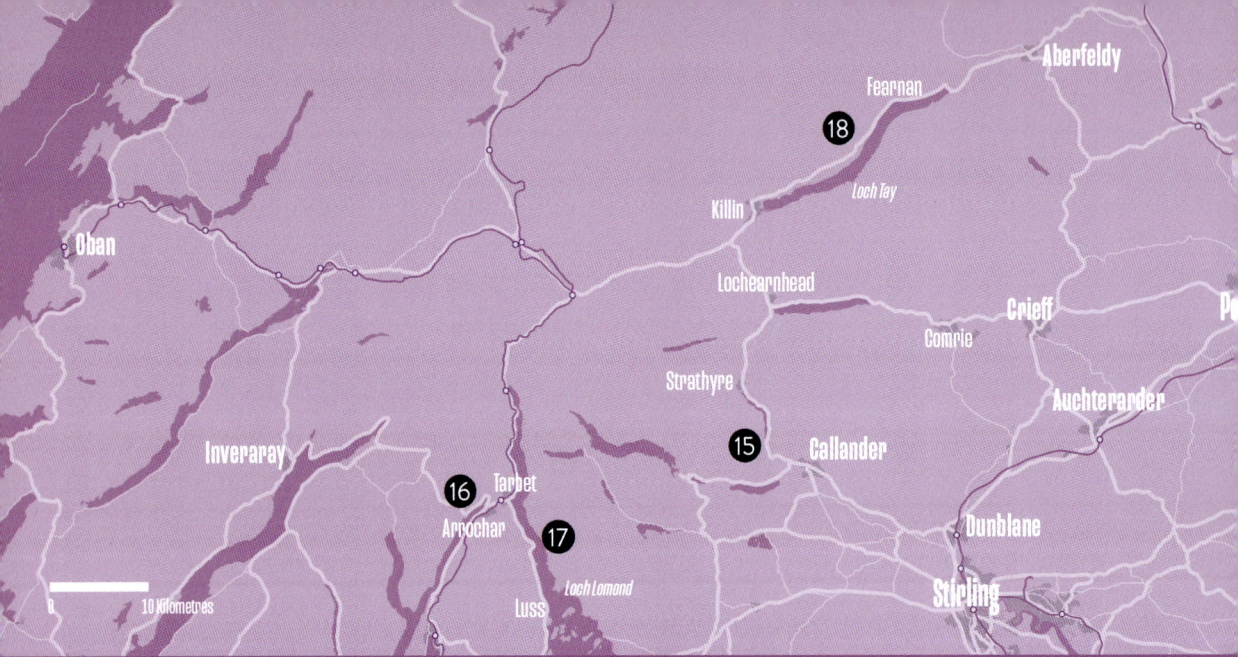

The Southern Highlands is a place of contrasts: the low hills of the Central Belt suddenly give way to towering giants; the populous towns bustle right next to vast wild places; green trees and deep lochs peel back to reveal chains of mountains.

For all these reasons, the Southern Highlands is a vibrant and diverse area for any outdoor lover. There are roads and trails just pining to be cycled, and enough rivers and lochs to entertain kayak or canoe enthusiasts for years.

For the runner, there are few places that can beat the Southern Highlands. While you have the lofty summit of Ben Lawers to draw the keen mountain runners, you have gentler hills and trails all around for anyone wanting to explore the world closer to sea level.

On a clear day, many of the summits in the region provide phenomenal views to the areas to the north, such as Glen Coe or the Cairngorms. Thanks to its glens and lochs, the hills can also be the scene of some of the most phenomenal cloud inversions – providing an amazing experience of being above the sea of cloud.

Nature is to be found everywhere, with eagles above, rare alpine plants on the ground and salmon in the waters.

I have tried to make the routes in this area as varied as possible so you can enjoy the best the Southern Highlands have to offer. Ben Lomond, The Cobbler and Ben Ledi all provide easily accessible, straightforward and fun trails; meanwhile, Ben Lawers and its neighbouring peaks provide an incredible day in the mountains, with opportunities to shorten or extend your adventure.

Other great hills in this area include Ben Vorlich and its neighbour Stùc a' Chroin, the Bridge of Orchy hills and some sublime trails in the Big Tree Country of Perthshire.

OPPOSITE *THE DESCENT FROM BEN LEDI* (ROUTE 15)

SOUTHERN HIGHLANDS

'Whether you're a seasoned fell runner or new to running, Ben Ledi has something for everyone. For me, the views are unrivalled with a 360-degree panoramic view of the Southern Highlands from the summit. A true adventurers' hill, which will keep you coming back for more.'   PETE COX

Pete is a Callander-based runner. He has raced the Ben Nevis Ultra and Ring of Steall Skyrace. He is happiest on big mountain days and running on technical ridges.

15
BEN LEDI
11km

The Trossachs is one of the most stunning areas in Central Scotland. Richly layered in beautiful woodlands, the Trossachs lies just to the east of Ben Lomond and is comprised of some of the loveliest lochs, glens and low hills this part of the country has to offer.

So tranquil is the area that Sir Walter Scott made a roll call to various spots in the Trossachs in his poem *The Lady of the Lake*. Away from poetry, the Trossachs is absolutely prime cycling, swimming and running country.

I am slightly biased. Having grown up in the neighbouring shire of Clackmannanshire, and having spent five years studying at Stirling University, I have spent a lot of time riding on the roads and running in the hills of this area.

One hill I and many others in the Stirling area come back to is Ben Ledi. Not achieving Munro status by a mere 35 metres, Ben Ledi – I believe – provides one of the best views in Central Scotland. From the summit, you can see out towards Edinburgh and Glasgow in the south, and north to the big lumps of the Southern Highlands – Ben Lui, Ben More, Ben Lawers, and so on. Sitting proudly above the town of Callander, its horned shape is visible from miles around.

The route has a recently revamped path for much of the way from the base to the summit, but the descent off the back, along its ridge and down into Stank Glen (a most wonderfully named glen; tragically, it didn't make it into Walter Scott's poetry) makes for an excellent twist on a popular route.

Distance 11km   **Ascent** 747m   **Time** 1–3 hours   **Start** Ben Ledi car park, A84   **Start latitude/longitude** 56.2533, -4.2823   **Start grid reference** NN 587091   **Difficulty** 1/5 – Easy trails and paths almost the entire way   **Bogs** 2/5 – Slightly wet on initial descent but almost devoid of bogs   **Terrain** Paths and trails   **Map** Harvey Superwalker, Ben Ledi & Hills North of Callander (1:25,000)

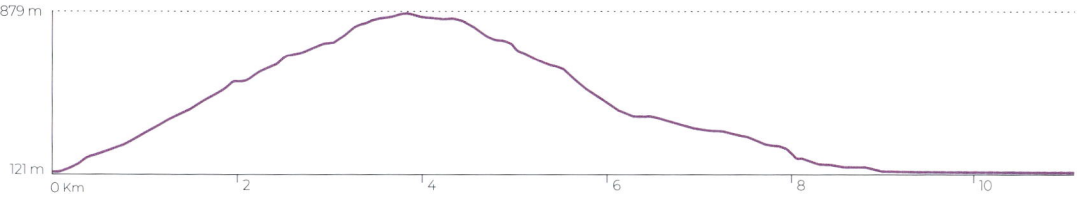

OPPOSITE *THE TRACK UP BEN LEDI*

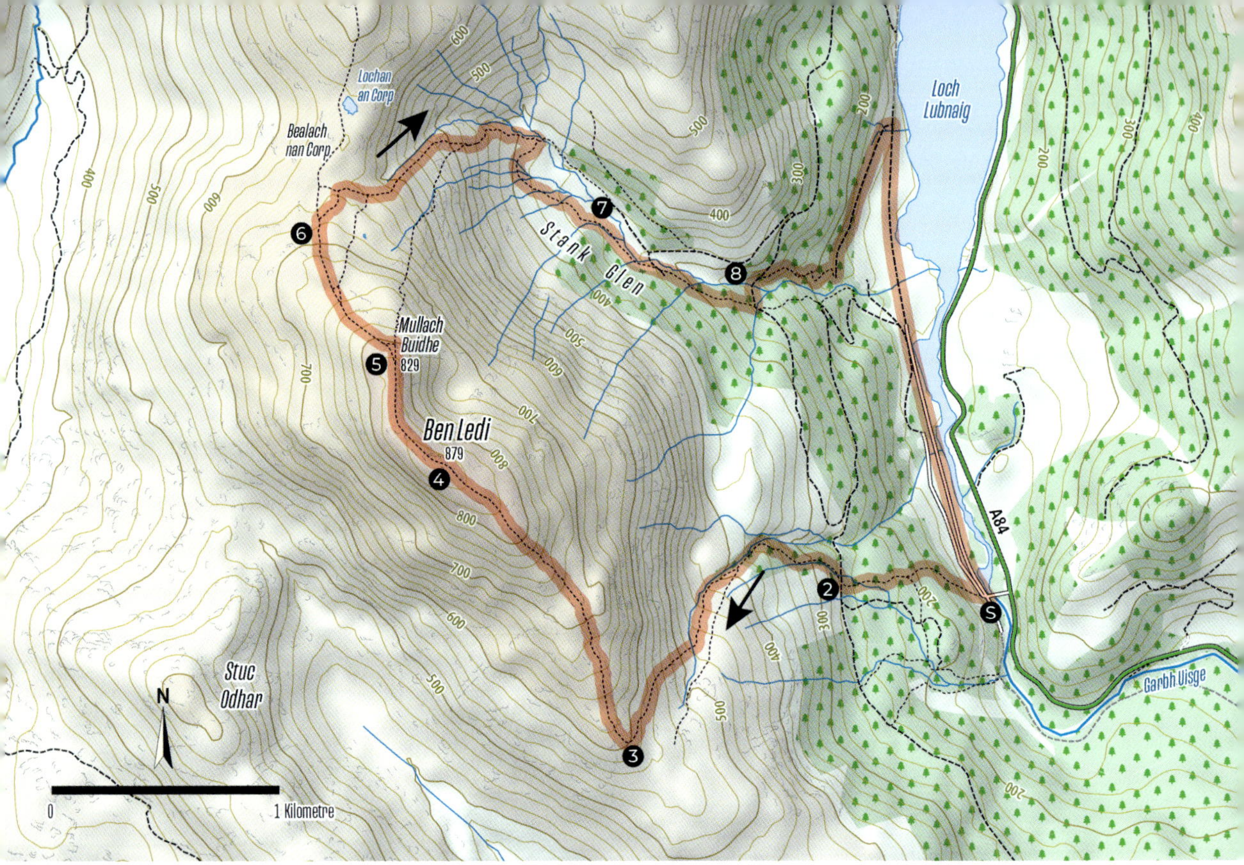

ON THE WAY UP BEN LEDI

THE TRACK INTO STANK GLEN

DIRECTIONS

S Leave the car park to reach the metal bridge you crossed to reach the car park. Don't cross the bridge; instead turn left then immediately fork left on to a gravel path, following the small wooden signpost for *Ben Ledi*. This climbs relatively steeply, giving you a cracking view over Loch Lubnaig. This is amazing on a cold dawn, as the mist hangs low over the loch.

2 Cross straight over a fire road and continue up the path, which has occasional steps to get you up the steep incline. As you emerge from the trees, you will see the path stretch out ahead of you, climbing on a consistent gradient the whole way.

3 Eventually you come to a corner on the trail where it curves round to head northwards. Immediately, the view expands to the south and west and continues to give you amazing vistas to the aspiringly titled Arrochar Alps and Ben Lomond in the west. The path climbs over two false summits before a final short climb up to the summit of Ben Ledi. The top is marked by a trig point, but the most obvious feature nearby is the giant cross. The cross is in memory of Sergeant Harry Lawrie, who died while on a call-out with the Killin Moutain Rescue Team in 1987.

4 Continue over the summit and follow the picturesque ridge over the back of Ben Ledi. The views here are just sensational. I love this section: the ridge ahead just seems to end, like you are about to jump into the big mountain landscape ahead of you.

5 Keep slightly left at the cairn at the end of the ridge and turn down to the left. Follow a series of old fenceposts all the way down into a wide saddle. The path can be a little wet in patches here.

6. Continue to descend until you come to a small pile of stones which marks the point you should turn right. (There are a number of faint paths you can take at this point to go right – the main thing is to turn right before you start heading uphill again.) Pass and cross a small stream before joining an excellent section of singletrack which snakes its way around the edge of the hillside before dropping into Stank Glen.

7. Follow the rocky path downhill, which eventually flattens out and enters a conifer plantation. Keep descending then turn left on to a fire road, which goes uphill slightly.

8. You will soon spot a blue waymarker and a signpost marking *Return to cabins*; turn right here, following the signpost. The path continues downhill, then you pop out at a little community hydro scheme where you turn left and follow a straight track down to the cabins. Turn right to join a tarmac road before turning right again and running the last 2km back to the start of the route.

LEFT HEADING FROM THE SUMMIT OF BEN LEDI TOWARDS THE RIDGE **BELOW LEFT** VIEWS ACROSS THE TROSSACHS **ABOVE** THE FINAL DESCENT

POINTS OF INTEREST
- **Corbett** Ben Ledi (Hill of the Slope), 879m

HIGHLIGHTS
- Excellent trail to the summit
- Fantastic views all around
- Easily accessible route
- Great singletrack trail before Stank Glen

GETTING THERE
Callander is roughly 5 kilometres from the start of the route – buses from Stirling stop here.

By bike, there is a very good cycle path from Callander, through Kilmahog, to the start of the route. This is part of National Cycle Network route 7, which heads to Strathyre, Killin and on to Inverness.

Alternatively, Ben Ledi car park is at the start of the route. Cross a metal bridge from the A84 and the car park is on your left. If this is full, there is some roadside parking on the A84 nearby.

TOP TIP
Ben Ledi is amazing for a sunrise or a sunset run. If it were me, I would go for sunrise, as Stank Glen is east facing and can get chilly after the sun dips behind the hill!

OTHER OPTIONS
One way to extend the route is to run along the boggy plateau over to Benvane. This is a fun extension but, as I say, can be a bit boggy even on a fairly dry day (21km; 1,163m ascent).

WHERE TO REFUEL
Callander is full of excellent little cafes and bakeries. Chief among them is **Mhor Bread** – the pies in here are to die for and the coffee is pretty good too. **Ben Ledi Coffee Company** also has great coffee, plus some quality brownies. There are also a few places for a bigger plate of food, like **Fat Jacks**, and, along the road, the **Lade Inn** is a superb pub.

'Despite its relatively low summit compared to nearby Munros, The Cobbler is as fine a running route as there is. Scottish climbing history was made here as Johnny Cunningham and Jock Nimlin created new routes in these crags and cliffs. It's a truly unique mountain.' GRAHAM KELLY (AKA BEARDY)

Graham is an all-round mountain man, based in Glasgow. He has a long history of mountaineering and climbing, has completed the Munros and the Corbetts, and nowadays enjoys hill running with a little graded scrambling thrown in. He is also a long-standing Mountain Rescue Team member.

16
THE COBBLER – BEN ARTHUR
11km

The Cobbler – otherwise known as Ben Arthur – is probably one of the most iconic and recognisable mountains south of the Highlands.

Its crooked smile of a shape can be seen from miles around; is so named because it looks like a cobbler (a shoemaker) bent over his machinery.

Despite it falling short of Munro status, The Cobbler is one of Scotland's most popular mountains, and with good reason: standing among the so-called Arrochar Alps, this Corbett gives fantastic views of its neighbouring Munros of Beinn Ime and Beinn Narnain, across Argyll and Bute and further to the Isle of Arran.

Argyll and Bute is part of an ancient Gaelic kingdom called Dál Riata, with Argyll translating to 'Coast of the Gaels' in Gaelic. The kingdom stretched from the coast of Northern Ireland and covered much of this area of Scotland, hence Scots Gaelic is traditionally spoken in this area as it is descended from Irish Gaelic.

Argyll and Bute boasts nearly 4,000 kilometres of coastline, 61 castles, 24 distilleries and 23 inhabited islands. In recent years, the group Wild About Argyll has worked hard to promote the area to visitors, so be sure to check out the rest of this fascinating area.

Distance 11km **Ascent** 884m **Time** 1–3 hours **Start** Succoth **Start latitude/longitude** 56.2061, -4.7503 **Start grid reference** NN 295049 **Difficulty** 2/5 – Almost entirely straightforward bar a small section of exposure at the start of the descent **Bogs** 2/5 – Entirely dry until the latter section of the descent which can be boggy after rain **Terrain** Paths with a grassy descent **Map** Harvey Superwalker, Arrochar Alps (1:25,000)

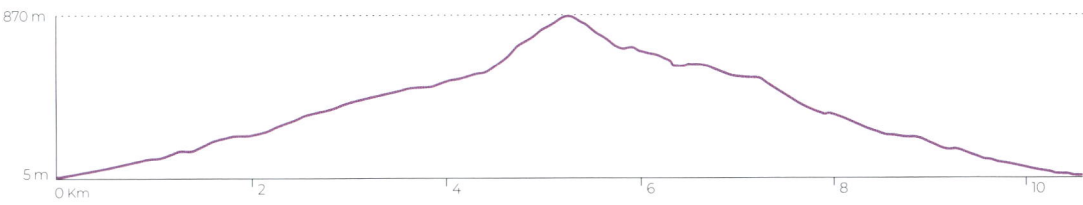

OPPOSITE *THE COBBLER*

DIRECTIONS

S The path starts opposite the car park in Succoth – follow the signpost for *Hill Access to Beinn Narnain and The Cobbler*. At the time of writing, there are some Portaloos at the start, with donations encouraged for their use. Start up this good path as it zigzags up the hill. Try to avoid cutting any corners as this is starting to cause erosion, which causes fast water run-off and more erosion as a result.

2 Turn left at a junction, where a signpost with a walker on it marks the way. Turn right at the next junction and head up into the forest. The zigzags are steep at times, so running may be more hands-on-knees, but as the trees are left behind the trail flattens out, giving way to some lovely runnable terrain. Very soon, the dramatic shape of The Cobbler appears ahead of you, with Beinn Narnain on its right.

3 Continue up the path, passing a small hydro dam – this is where you will cross the river on your descent.

4 Around 1.5km after the hydro dam, the path splits. Turn left to ascend steeply up the rocky steps to reach the bealach between The Cobbler and North Peak. (Alternatively, go right at the junction to another bealach before turning left to reach North Peak and the bealach beyond – this option adds around 0.6km of running.)

5 Turn left up the easy-gradient path, soon cresting on to the summit plateau. The 'actual' summit is the rather precarious-looking stack of rock in front of you, which requires a butt-clenching climb through a hole and on to its top. It isn't for the faint-hearted, so you can just admire the efforts of others attempting it.

6 To descend, walk towards the stone stack and look to your right to see a worn path descending around the base of it. Take this

ABOVE *LOOKING BACK DOWN THE PATH* **BELOW** *FOLLOW THE WHITE WAYMARKERS*

16 THE COBBLER – BEN ARTHUR

and join the ridge. At one point, it looks like you are about to traverse a sketchy terrace, but thankfully you drop down again to the right on another path. Make your way down the at-times-awkward boulders until the path levels out and becomes grassy. Take a moment to look behind you to admire this angle of The Cobbler, which looks seriously impressive. Follow the rolling grassy ridge downhill, with Loch Long stretching out ahead of you.

❼ Once you've covered around 2km from the summit, the path veers left towards the river. This section can be very boggy after rain. Reach the river and cross at the hydro dam to join the trail you ascended on. After that, it's a quick descent on excellent trails back to the start of the route.

LEFT *THE COBBLER'S SUMMIT STACK*   **ABOVE** *THE COBBLER*
BELOW *LOCH LONG*

POINTS OF INTEREST
- **Corbett** The Cobbler (Ben Arthur), 884m
- Loch Long

HIGHLIGHTS
- Running an iconic mountain
- Great trails to the summit
- Lovely grassy ridge to descend
- Picturesque views across Argyll

GETTING THERE
Buses run to Arrochar from Glasgow in the south and Oban in the north. There is a railway station between Arrochar and Tarbet for easy rail connections.

Alternatively, there are two car parks (both pay and display) on the A83 at Succoth and Arrochar. It works out better to be a runner as the charges are by the hour!

TOP TIP
The Cobbler is a stunning mountain and very accessible. For that reason, it is busy at peak times, so think about ways to avoid the busyness by taking the bus, cycling, or going later in the day.

OTHER OPTIONS
If you want a different option, you can't go far wrong with adding Beinn Narnain to the loop. Start as for the main route and soon turn right. Strike up this path on a quad-burning ascent. Pass the old concrete block of an old railway used for the hydro scheme at Loch Sloy, eventually coming to the 926-metre summit of Beinn Narnain. Cross the summit and drop to the path junction at its base. Now head up The Cobbler and descend via the grassy ridge (11km; 1,193m ascent).

WHERE TO REFUEL
The **Bonnie and Ben Cafe** is located just a short distance away in Tarbet, with great views across Scotland's most famous loch – Loch Lomond.

LOVED THIS ROUTE?
The Friends of Loch Lomond and the Trossachs raise money for the natural and cultural heritage of the national park. Learn more at **www.lochlomondtrossachs.org.uk**

16 THE COBBLER – BEN ARTHUR

'Scotland's most southerly Munro, Ben Lomond, was a memorable hill on our Munro Round – and not just because of the rare dry and sunny weather! Accessible, yet adventurous, Ben Lomond's airy ridge offers amazing views and fun, easy scrambling. The fast, flowy descent is excellent fun.' LIBBY JONES AND LISA WATSON

Libby and Lisa are two Peak-District-based runners who set the women's record for the Munro Round in 2017 in 77 days.

17
BEN LOMOND VIA THE PTARMIGAN RIDGE
12km

Ask anyone to name a mountain in Scotland and it's very likely that, alongside Ben Nevis, they will include Ben Lomond. Around 30,000 people per year clamber on to this prominent peak, following the straightforward track from the base to the summit.

Its location not far from Glasgow partly explains its popularity. In addition, its proximity to the West Highland Way and position above Scotland's most famous loch – Loch Lomond – are big draws; the whole area is a hub for runners, walkers, cyclists and water sports enthusiasts. However, the route I have for you takes you up a slightly less conventional way, which affords you a feeling of relative solitude and adventure over Ben Lomond's western ridge.

The Ptarmigan and its ridge are named after the furtive bird of the same name. The Gaelic *tarmachan* actually translates to 'croaker', after its recognisable croaking call. These plump birds look a lot like grouse but only waddle around in the higher mountains, above around 900 metres.

In winter, their granite-coloured plumage is replaced by pure white feathers, allowing them to blend into their snowy surroundings (though, given Scotland's temperamental winters, they often stick out like a sore thumb).

The other bonus to this ridge is the sublime views it gives as you run above Loch Lomond, with uninterrupted views to the Arrochar Alps in the west and north to the Highlands.

On the way back, you get a fast, flowy descent past all the walkers wondering how you got there before them!

Distance 12km **Ascent** 971m **Time** 1–3 hours **Start** Rowardennan **Start latitude/longitude** 56.1518, -4.6418 **Start grid reference** NS 360986 **Difficulty** 2/5 – Slight scramble at the top but almost entirely on good paths and trails **Bogs** 1/5 – Almost entirely on dry trails, even after rain **Terrain** Paths and trails **Map** Harvey Superwalker, Loch Lomond & the Trossachs (1:25,000)

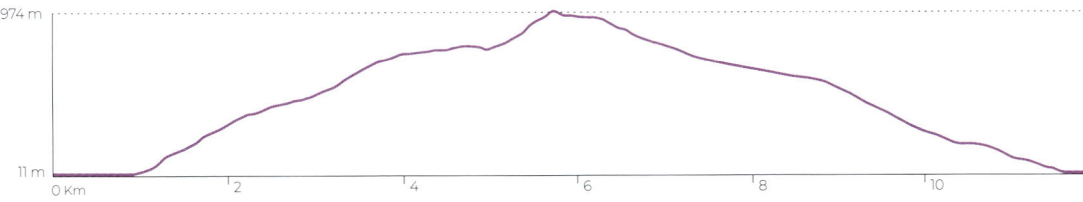

OPPOSITE *MAIN PATH UP BEN LOMOND* © PAUL WEBSTER

STONE STEPS NEAR THE END OF THE ROUTE © PAUL WEBSTER

106 RUNNING ADVENTURES SCOTLAND

LOCH LOMOND © PAUL WEBSTER

MAIN PATH UP BEN LOMOND © PAUL WEBSTER

DIRECTIONS

S On a nice day, the initial part of the run is lovely in itself. When you come back, I highly recommend a dip in the loch – a blessing for anyone who takes on the brutally fast Ben Lomond Hill Race. Head north from Rowardennan, following the shoreline and joining the West Highland Way. Pass the Rowardennan Lodge Youth Hostel on your left and enter the beautiful woodland that adorns the entirety of this side of the loch. Continue up the main track, ignoring the first right-hand track to Ardress Lodge. Soon after, in the woods, you will see a path head off to the right, likely with a marker indicating *Ptarmigan Path*; naturally, this is your route.

2 The path heads up through the woodland, zigzagging up until you clear the trees and are on the open hillside. Now's the chance to start taking in the views, which only improve the higher you go. It's a clear, well-maintained path the whole way, so there should be no issues with navigation. For the first few

LOCH LOMOND'S MANY ISLANDS © PAUL WEBSTER

kilometres you run along the hillside, before a steep section at 500m elevation takes you up on to the Ptarmigan Ridge itself.

❸ Here the views are fantastic, and you get a unique view of the impressive lump that is Ben Lomond above you. You'll likely see tiny figures crawling up it on the main tourist path. Follow the path over the summit of Ptarmigan.

❹ After the summit of Ptarmigan, the path slowly bends to the right to the foot of a very steep climb to the summit of the Ben itself. This does involve a small amount of scrambling, but nothing too daring.

❺ You will soon pop out on to the summit of the Ben and startle everyone who will wonder how on earth you got there. Take in the surrounding views of Loch Lomond and the Arrochar Alps in the west, the Trossachs to the east and Greater Glasgow to the south. It's a really unique view – a meeting point of wilderness and mankind. Head off the summit and follow the path as it slowly bends to the left. Soon, it descends steeply on to a very runnable trail that slopes gently downwards. This is some really exhilarating running, if your legs have some steam left in them.

❻ Keep heading south, watching your feet in parts where the ground is rough. You will begin turning towards Loch Lomond, dropping steeply down to a gate before continuing on an obvious path over a river and through another gate. Cross straight over a connecting forest track and down on the most technical part of the descent with some steep boulder steps and some cobbled sections. Eventually, you pop out in a mad sprint finish at the visitor centre, legs suitably bashed after over 900m of descent and ready for a dip in the loch.

POINTS OF INTEREST
- **Munro** Ben Lomond (Beacon Hill), 974m
- **Summit** Ptarmigan, 731m
- Loch Lomond

HIGHLIGHTS
- Variation of an iconic route
- Excellent views up and down Loch Lomond
- Fast descent down the main path of Ben Lomond

GETTING THERE
There are no practical public transport options for this route.

The Ben Lomond car park (pay and display) is at the start of the route. It is often busy, so park considerately.

TOP TIP
The parking for Ben Lomond does get busy – get there early or go late to avoid the busiest times. Or you could consider parking at Balmaha then cycling on to Rowardennan to avoid missing that last parking spot!

OTHER OPTIONS
The straightforward way to do the Ben is up and down the tourist path. From the car park, go through the visitor centre and the path heads up from there – you can't go wrong (12km; 952m ascent).

WHERE TO REFUEL
The **Clansman Bar** at the Rowardennan Hotel is the closest spot to refuel and does do some darn good grub. When I ran the West Highland Way, they gave us a hearty breakfast and a packed lunch to see us on our way! Further back along the road, **St Mocha Coffee Shop and Ice Cream Parlour** does some *amazing* toasties and, naturally, pretty good ice cream.

LOVED THIS ROUTE?
The Friends of Loch Lomond and the Trossachs raise money for the natural and cultural heritage of the national park. Learn more at **www.lochlomondtrossachs.org.uk**

'The Lawers range has a bit of everything I enjoy about hill running: rocky paths, runnable climbs, rocky, steep climbs (An Stùc), bogs and amazing views. The range is perfect for a long day out in the hills, or you can head up Ben Lawers itself for a quick mountain run.' JILL STEPHEN

Jill is a Scottish hill running champion and coach based in Edinburgh. One of her favourite races is the Scottish Islands Peaks Race as it is a mini adventure. She loves steep, rocky climbs and eating chips.

18
BEN LAWERS
22km

The Ben Lawers range is widely seen as the first of the big mountain ranges on your way into the Highlands. Sat on the banks of Loch Tay, Ben Lawers is Scotland's tenth-highest Munro, standing at 1,214 metres.

The route I have for you is an absolute cracker; rarely straying too far below 1,000 metres in height, you will find all the aspects of a glorious mountain day as you visit the five Munros along the ridge, with steep sides, a graded scramble and some awe-inspiring trails.

At the foot of the Lawers range lies Loch Tay, the largest freshwater body in Perth and Kinross and the sixth largest in Scotland. Out of it flows the River Tay, Scotland's longest river, running for 190 kilometres all the way from Ben Lui to Dundee and the Firth of Tay.

Ben Lawers is within striking distance of Perth and Stirling, making it easily accessible from the city, but also close to the picturesque towns of Killin, Aberfeldy and Pitlochry. The area is lovely to visit at any time, but autumn is a real treat for all the colourful trees.

Given its altitude, and the area's status as a National Nature Reserve, you can expect a wide variety of flora and fauna in these high mountains. Foremost, the plants in the reserve are what make it so special, with the most extensive arctic–alpine flora in Britain.

Alpine plants such as alpine gentian, mountain sandwort and endangered species like rock lady's-mantle and alpine pearlwort all adorn this area. They join wildlife including ptarmigan, snow bunting, ring ouzel and mountain hare.

Distance 22km **Ascent** 1,786m **Time** 4–6 hours **Start** Lawers **Start latitude/longitude** 56.5288, -4.1525 **Start grid reference** NN 677395 **Difficulty** 3/5 – Contains one grade 1 scramble and some steep climbs **Bogs** 2/5 – Final descent can be soft underfoot, but the ridge is bog-free **Terrain** A bit of everything **Map** Harvey Ultramap, Ben Lawers & Schiehallion (1:40,000)

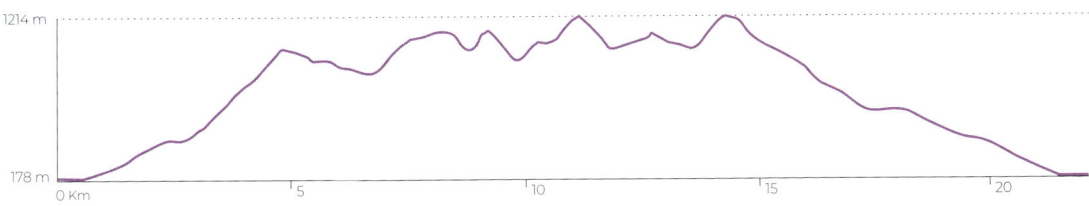

OPPOSITE *LOOKING OVER LOCH TAY FROM MEALL GREIGH*

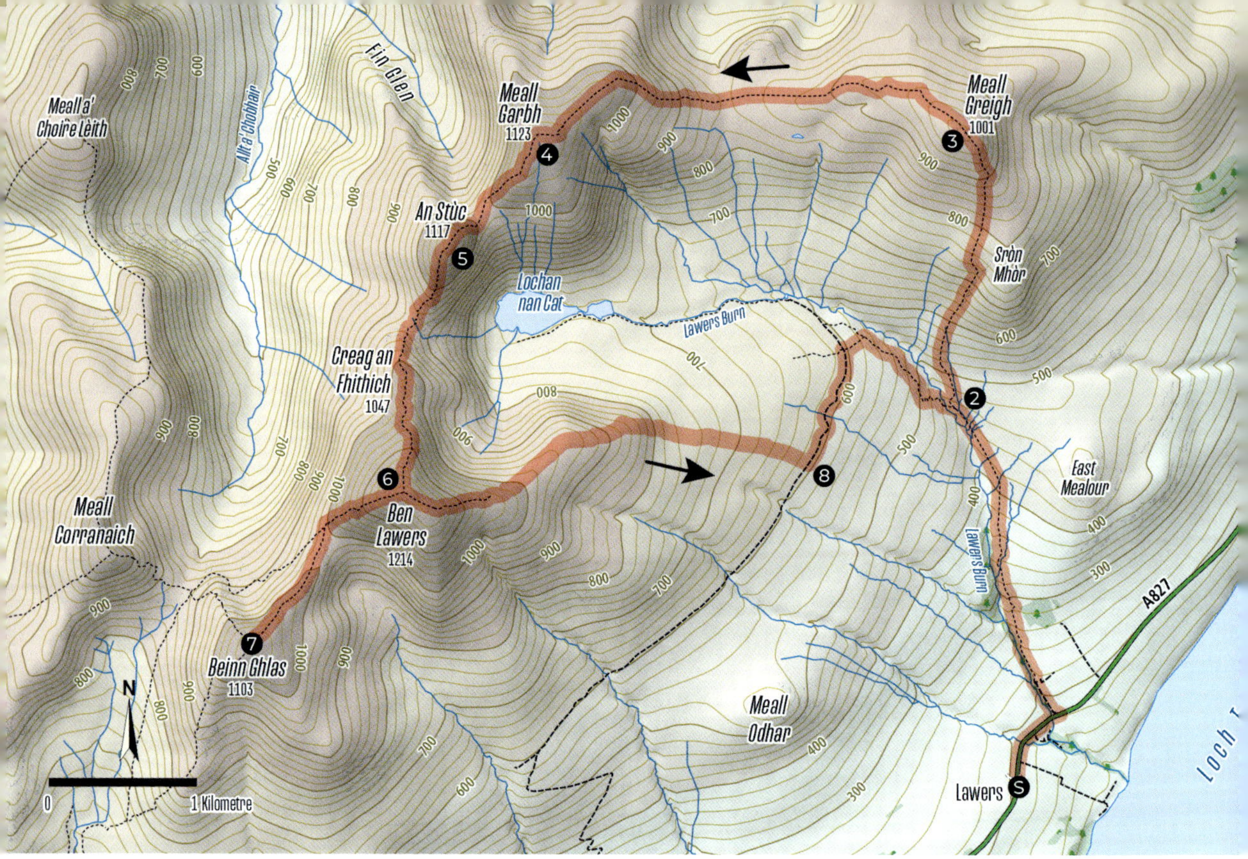

LOCH TAY CLOUD INVERSION FROM CAT GULLY

ASCENDING MEALL GREIGH

DIRECTIONS

S Once at the Ben Lawers Hotel, enjoy its high vantage point across Loch Tay. Jog downhill heading east across a bridge and pass the horn carving workshop, with its unique array of carvings outside. Just after the workshop, turn left to begin heading uphill alongside the Lawers Burn and enter a woodland. Once you pop out of the woods again, take a moment to look over your shoulder to the increasingly impressive vista of the Southern Highlands. To the south you might spot the dome of Ben Vorlich and its neighbour Stùc a' Chroin; to the west rises the 'Big Hill' Ben More and its pal Stob Binnein. The ground at the foot of Meall Greigh is littered with old shielings. These are buildings used by people in bygone days when they moved their sheep and cattle up the hill in summer to enjoy the lush grasses. Keep to the Lawers Burn heading towards the corrie.

2 Around 2.5km into the run, follow the path which shoots away to the right up the steep side of Meall Greigh, which is the first Munro of the day.

3 Despite its lack of fame, Meall Greigh has a great position on the range as a prominent viewpoint with no obstructions to the view across the Tay Valley. After soaking it in, cross the summit and bear left to head towards the second Munro – Meall Garbh – which is reached by following a long fence line heading west. This view is really cool: you get a superb shot across the rest of the ridge, with the unambiguously titled An Stùc – The Peak – ahead of you, and beyond that the towering figure of Ben Lawers.

4 The path down Meall Garbh is a little eroded, so just mind your step although it will keep your attention from the formidable-looking climb up An Stùc. Luckily, it isn't as hard as it looks. The main route starts up a tight zigzag path before keeping to the left up a short, grade 1 scramble, which is the crux of the climb. For the faint-hearted this may be daunting; a bypass can be made around the right-hand side of the crags, but this can hold on to snow for a while through spring. Once past the crux, the ground to the summit is easy enough, and you get the

MEALL GARBH

fabulous feeling of being on a prominent peak nestled among high mountains.

5 The south-west side of An Stùc is far easier than the north-east, so the descending is great fun. Drop into the bealach and begin the long climb up Ben Lawers. Keep right at a set of boulders to avoid an unnecessary climb and follow the good path all the way to the 1,214m summit. I hope you get good weather, because wow! I have been on Ben Lawers many times and it never gets old – especially if you get a cloud inversion. The route can be left here if you are satisfied, but there's a chance to nab a fifth Munro – Beinn Ghlas – which is just a short jaunt away.

6 Descend Ben Lawers on a steep, stone-pitched path heading west and keep left at a fork. The path gradually ascends Beinn Ghlas. You can see the Bridge of Balgie road below with the main Ben Lawers car park. Directly across is another lovely ridge – Meall nan Tarmachan.

7 Head back to the bealach and climb back up Ben Lawers. To get back to the start, turn right at the summit cairn to head east to a prominent spur. Follow the shoulder of the hill downhill, keeping Lochan nan Cat on your left. There is a faint path for 500m, but eventually you have to make your way across grassy ground to the vehicle track below.

8 Turn left to follow the track along the hillside heading north-east, back towards the Lawers Burn, at which point you turn right to descend back into the forest and back to the start of the route.

LEFT *BEN LAWERS FROM BEINN GHLAS*   ABOVE *RETURN FROM BEINN GHLAS*

POINTS OF INTEREST
- **Munro** Meall Greigh (Round Hill of the Horse Stud), 1,001m
- **Munro** Meall Garbh (Rough Rounded Hill), 1,123m
- **Munro** An Stùc (The Peak), 1,117m
- **Munro** Ben Lawers (Hill of the Hoof), 1,214m
- **Munro** Beinn Ghlas (Grey-Green Hill), 1,103m

HIGHLIGHTS
- The stunning ridge
- Chance to do some scrambling
- Variety of the terrain
- Stunning views around you for the whole route

GETTING THERE
There are no practical public transport options for this route.

There is a car park is situated in the hamlet of Lawers by the Ben Lawers Hotel. The hotel has a money box outside to pay for parking, but it can be tight in high season.

TOP TIP
Being right next to a large body of water, Ben Lawers often gets amazing cloud inversions in the colder months.

OTHER OPTIONS
Ben Lawers and Beinn Ghlas can be climbed by themselves from the main Ben Lawers car park in the west as a simple loop (11km; 884m ascent). Follow the Burn of Edramucky to the bealach between the two Munros and ascend Ben Lawers before going back via Beinn Ghlas.

All seven Munros in the range can be completed from the northern hamlet of Invervar. It's a big day out over some rough ground, but is massively rewarding. The route heads up Meall Greigh and follows the ridge to Beinn Ghlas, before dropping down and then over the final two peaks of Meall Corranaich and Meall a' Choire Lèith (31km; 1,974m ascent).

WHERE TO REFUEL
Killin has a few little gems for you to refuel after your grand day out – **Shutters** does a great filled roll and pot of tea. To the east of Loch Tay in Aberfeldy, **Habitat Cafe** is one of my favourites – the coffee is exquisite and the cakes are divine. 'Feldy (as it is known) also has a great chippy, if you are a little late.

LOVED THIS ROUTE?
Much of this area is managed by the National Trust for Scotland. Head over to **www.nts.org.uk** to find out more.

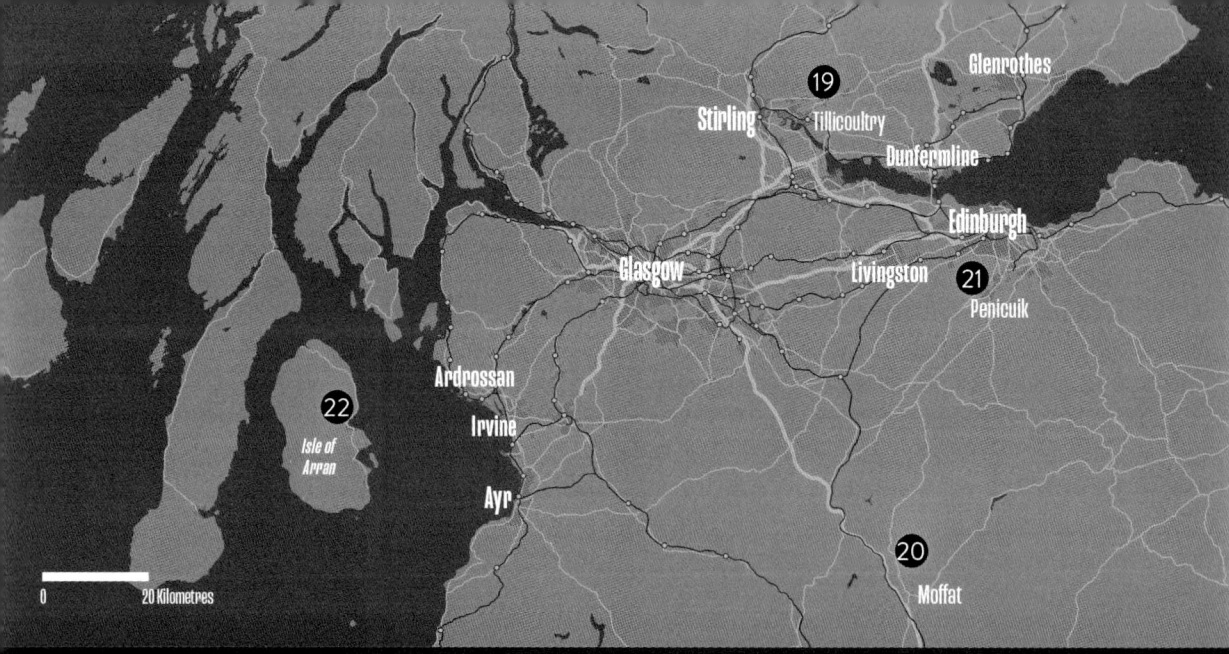

When we think of Scotland, our imaginations are instantly drawn to the Highlands. The Highland Boundary Fault, a tectonic fault line, cuts the country from Arran to Stonehaven, through places such as Aberfoyle, Crieff and Blairgowrie.

Yet, upon closer inspection, you will notice that a whole chunk of the country lies south of this line. While somewhat uncelebrated, the Central Belt and Southern Scotland have some of the finest, purest hill running in the country. I am biased, because I grew up at the foot of the Ochil Hills and I will always love running in them. It is home to some of the best-loved hill races in the Scottish calendar: Dumyat, Pentland Skyline, Tinto, Two Breweries and more besides.

Due to the area's relative lack of high peaks, ridges and steep bealachs, this is a great place to get some actual running in, and can provide an excellent challenge to both novice and experienced trail and hill runners. With hills easily accessed from the city, you can quickly nip out and enjoy a feeling of adventure in just a few kilometres.

Historically, Central and Southern Scotland were home to Scotland's industries: coal, textiles and shipbuilding. It is also farming country, with fertile soils and rolling plains. If you have time between your running endeavours, you can visit Edinburgh and Stirling castles, the Wallace Monument, Bannockburn, North Berwick and, of course, breweries galore!

The routes in this book are all easily accessible from the south or Scotland's main cities. The Pentland Skyline is a classic route, and on the doorstep of the capital, while the Moffat Hills provide a neat adventure next to the A74(M). A mini adventure to this section's island, Arran, beckons and, naturally, I had to feature my favourite hills: the Ochils.

BEALACH BETWEEN CIR MHÒR AND NORTH GOATFELL (ROUTE 22) © TOM FELLBAUM

CENTRAL & SOUTHERN
SCOTLAND

'I have loved living with the Ochils on my doorstep for 50 years. They have everything a hill runner needs: thigh-burning climbs, miles of lovely, rolling grassy paths and beautiful hidden glens. Despite being within an hour of most of Scotland's population, they are seldom busy and definitely my happy place.' KATY BAXTER

Katy is a Tillicoultry-based hill runner and cyclist, and is the chair of the Ochil Hill Runners, the local running club.

19 HEART OF THE OCHILS

12km

Having grown up at the foot of the Ochils, they have been my playground for many years, so I have come to know them quite well. I may be biased, but the Ochil Hills are one of the most fantastic places to get into hill running and to train for almost any challenge, be it long and lumpy, short and steep or navigation-based.

Located in Clackmannanshire, the Ochils are positioned in Scotland's Central Belt and are easily accessible from Edinburgh and Glasgow. Nearby Stirling is a historic city, once home to James VI (of Scotland) and I (of England). The Hillfoots Villages of Tillicoultry, Alva and Dollar were well known for their mills, powered by the water that flows from the hills.

Though reaching a modest maximum height of 721 metres, the Ochils play host to a wide array of weather and wildlife. Typically smothered in clag, these hills can be blanketed with deep snow in winter or baked in sunshine in summer. In the spring and summer, they are full of skylarks chirruping incessantly and, in winter, you might see migratory birds like snow bunting and fieldfares. When the air is clear, you can see north into the Cairngorms and the distinctive shape of Ben Lomond in the west.

This loop takes in one of my favourite routes, with lots of options to add bits on or cut it shorter. It is very runnable and takes you over the highest point in the range – Ben Cleuch. As a nice touch, the route traces a heart shape – hence the title.

Distance 12km   **Ascent** 784m   **Time** 1–3 hours   **Start** Tillicoultry   **Start latitude/longitude** 56.1569, -3.7484   **Start grid reference** NS 915974   **Difficulty** 1/5 – Very smooth ground and quite clear paths all around with some steep climbs   **Bogs** 2/5 – Ground can be quite soft in places, but not much in way of bog   **Terrain** Grassy the whole way   **Map** Harvey Superwalker, Ochil Hills (1:25,000)

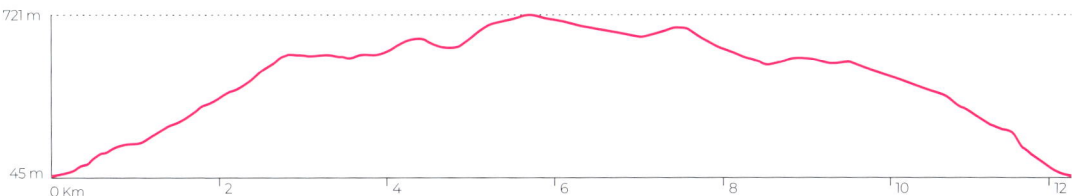

OPPOSITE *METAL BRIDGE IN MILL GLEN*

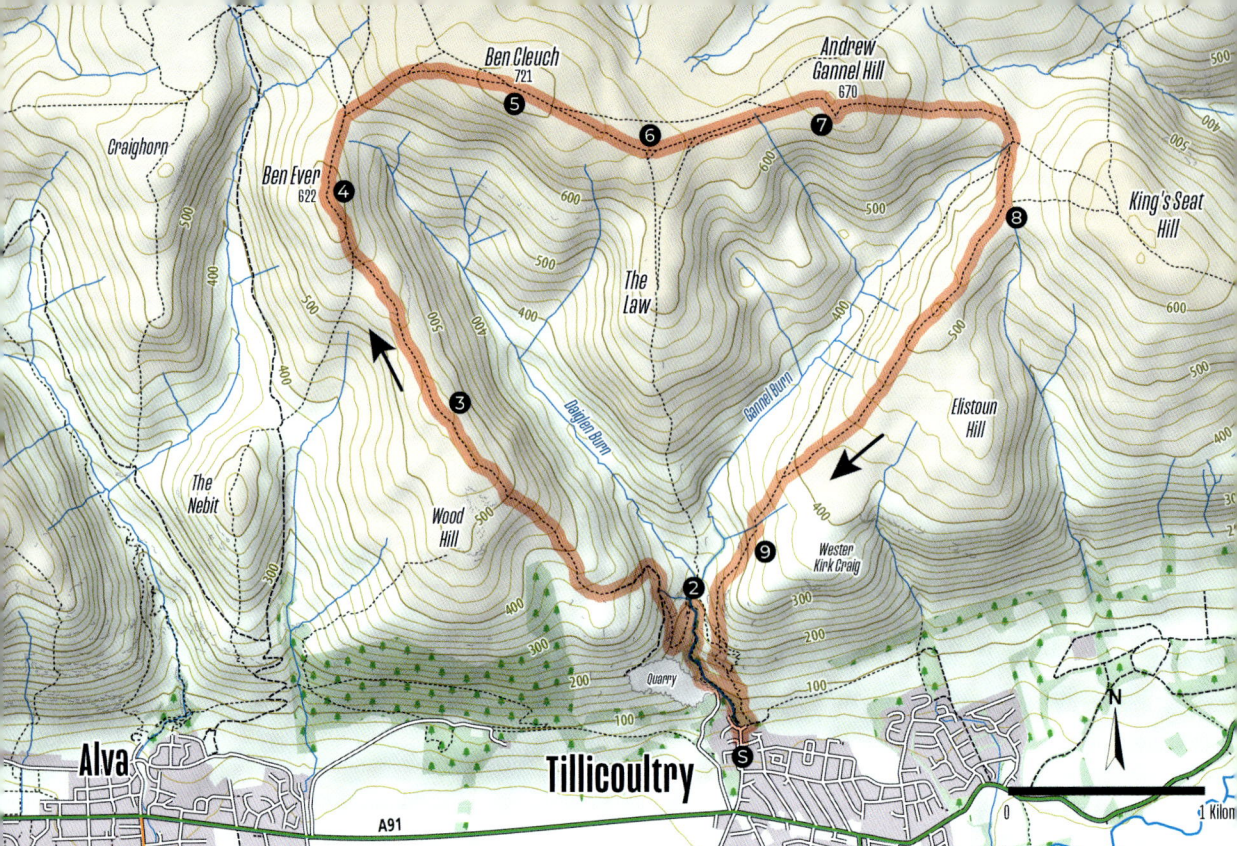

DIRECTIONS

S If you are coming to Tillicoultry in spring, lucky you. Upper Mill Street is graced by dozens of blossom trees that burst into pale pink at this time of year. Run up the road towards, and past, a short set of steps. Keep heading up, following the river and passing through a small metal gate. From here, continue up Mill Glen on the path which snakes its way up a deep gorge, crossing the river several times. Climb a set of steep wooden stairs on the right of the river and cross the river again on a metal bridge.

2 Here the path splits. To the right is a steep set of steps but you should keep left, where a set of zigzags becomes a path that runs above the gorge you have just ascended. Follow this path for 100m until you see a path going up to the right. Head up this path, briefly following the fence line that surrounds the disused Tillicoultry Quarry, before the path hairpins right, eventually leading you to a large cairn. The Ochil Hills now really do rise up around you, with The Law the most prominent, flanked by Andrew Gannel Hill on the right and Ben Cleuch's bump on the left. Follow the clear grassy path uphill for 1.3km, where you eventually reach a fence line and a plateau. Phew – it's a long climb!

3 Once on the plateau, follow the fence line north, hopefully admiring the sloping top of Ben Cleuch on your right. You also get an ace view out to Ben Lomond in the west from here, easy spotted due to its classic pointed mountain shape. Keep following the path north to eventually reach a gradual uphill slope. This takes you to the summit of Ben Ever.

4 Ben Ever is underrated, in my opinion. It has phenomenal views of the more southerly Munros of Scotland, including Ben Vorlich and Stùc a' Chroin, as well as to the Arrochar Alps and the weirdly shaped Cobbler. Follow the path off the summit which bends to the right into a shallow bealach. Cross the stile, and start the long, steep climb up the side

THE LAW

of Ben Cleuch, following the fence. Near the top, the path bends away from the fence, heading right on gradually rising ground. The summit of Ben Cleuch is soon reached; it features a cairn, trig point and a map with all the surrounding summits named, which I love staring at.

❺ Continue along the path which slowly descends, again following a long fence. In winter, I enjoy coming here as the fence usually looks like a long line of waffles made of snow. This part of the route can be quite boggy; the path jumps left and right in an attempt to avoid the worst parts.

❻ Around 800m from the top of Ben Cleuch the path splits. (The path on the right leads to The Law; you can do an out-and-back to The Law (which adds around 1.1km to the route), or continue on from The Law to cut the route short.) To stay on the main route, keep left and cross the stile. Head east, following – you guessed it – another long fence. You drop into a steep-sided marsh en route to Andrew Gannel Hill, but there are some planks handily placed to allow you to skip across the bog. Ascend gradually to the summit plateau of Andrew Gannel Hill. Turn right and the summit is at the edge of a steep drop.

❼ Here you get a great view south over the Forth Valley, out to the River Forth and beyond to Edinburgh and the Pentland Hills; you can even see Bass Rock on a good day. Leave your climbing legs here. From Andrew Gannel Hill to the finish there is only one small uphill section; the rest is quite possibly the most enjoyable and runnable descent in the world! I don't think that's an exaggeration … Turn left from the summit and begin descending on a smooth path all the way down into a steep col. This bit is also quite boggy. Once you make your way around it, take the path on the left that heads uphill for a short while.

ABOVE *RUNNING TOWARDS BEN EVER* BELOW *BEN CLEUCH SUMMIT* © GRANT BAXTER RIGHT *DAIGLEN BURN*

❽ At the top, join the main path that heads to the right. Follow this. It starts a bit flat and bumpy but turns into the most amazing descent. Pass a small cairn and keep dropping down. Watch your feet as you see an old fence line – there can be old post stumps in the ground that can cause a rather nasty face plant. Down, down you go, crossing a small stream. The last part of the descent is a bit rough, over lots of rocks stuck in the ground. Eventually, the path bends left, and you find a large boulder in the middle of the path. This is a nice point to stretch out your hamstrings from all that descending – because you're about to do some more.

❾ Continue on your trajectory, heading south. Pass a bench that overlooks the fields below. You have a choice here whether to follow the direct paths down the hill (as is shown on the map and in the GPX file) or follow the gently zigzagging path. Either way, keep the steep gorge on your right, heading to the fence below. To the far right of the fence is a walkers' gate where you enter a thickly wooded area. Head down the stepped path through the wood and emerge on a gravel farm track. Turn right and you are back at the start. Now look at your GPS trace and you will see why I call it the Heart of the Ochils.

THE OCHILS IN WINTER © GRANT BAXTER

POINTS OF INTEREST
- **Donald** Ben Cleuch, 721m
- **Summit** Andrew Gannel Hill, 670m
- **Summit** The Law, 638m
- **Summit** Ben Ever, 622m

HIGHLIGHTS
- The central location of the Ochil Hills
- Amazing descents
- Excellent route for trail runners looking to get into the hills
- Panoramic views north to the Cairngorms, Glen Coe and Ben Lomond

GETTING THERE
The route starts on Upper Mill Street, Tillicoultry. Buses run to Tillicoultry from Stirling, where there are onward connections to Edinburgh and Perth. The nearest railway station to the route is in Alloa; bus connections are available to Tillicoultry. Alternatively, on-street parking is available in Tillicoultry.

TOP TIP
Fancy a challenge? The Ochil Hills feature some classic races such as Run of the Mill, Maddy Moss and the Ochil 2000s. Come back and try them out!

OTHER OPTIONS
To shorten the route, from point **6** simply run south towards The Law and descend off the other side. This drops steeply down and, at the bottom, features a very short easy scramble down to the bridge. From there, climb up the railed path, turning left to skirt the hillside and eventually descend (10km; 742m ascent), or turn right to drop back into the gorge (10km; 736m ascent).

To lengthen the route, you can tap Ben Buck or King's Seat Hill. To reach Ben Buck, descend Ben Ever into the bealach. Instead of heading up the steep slope towards Ben Cleuch, cross the left-hand fence, and follow a faint trail up to the summit of Ben Buck. At the top, turn right to head south, following the fence up to the plateau of Ben Cleuch.

To add King's Seat Hill, descend Andrew Gannel Hill and, at the boggy section, immediately head straight ahead uphill, crossing a fence, and head directly up the faint path. Keep heading south-east, eventually reaching a flat summit area. The true summit is a quick out-and-back along the path. To descend, if coming from the summit, take the path to the left of the path you ascended on. The path drops down to a fence. Cross this and pick up the main route.

WHERE TO REFUEL
Tilly Tearoom in Tillicoultry has become quite the pitstop of late. Its selection of filled rolls, homemade cakes, soups and tea are excellent grub after a run in the hills.

LOVED THIS ROUTE?
Friends of the Ochils have done great work to promote and protect the Ochil Hills. Learn more at **www.friendsoftheochils.org.uk**

'Above Moffat's sleepy rooftops, I can spy the etched skyline of the Moffat Hills – Hart Fell; Whitehope Heights; Annanhead Hill. Over the round and proud summit of Hart Fell, the grassy ridge descends to the amphitheatre of the Devil's Beef Tub. With my collie companion smiling beside me, I remember why I love to call this place home.' RORY LONGMORE

Rory is a Beattock-based hill runner and cyclist, who loves the Border Hills and Lakeland Fells. With a 61-peak 24-hour Lakes run and three Fred Whitton sportives to his name, he loves hill racing in new places and ripping it up at the local Parkrun.

20
HART FELL HORSESHOE
17km

The area of Scotland close to the border with England is one of deep history. Dubbed the 'Debatable Lands', the line that now rests between Scotland and England shifted constantly during the Middle Ages, as warring factions gained and lost ground to one another. Meanwhile, clans and raiders, some known as the Border Reivers, made their strongholds here, making for a fascinating cultural landscape. One famous Scottish king is heavily connected with the area – Robert the Bruce – whose family reigned as the Lords of Annandale, and whose story is much connected to the area.

The hills of Southern Scotland are often neglected as visitors from south of the border just pass through the area on their way north, but they make for an excellent adventure, either on foot or by bike. As far as running goes, this route offers an excellent taste of some classic Scottish hill running, without having to travel too far north. With grassy, rolling slopes, Hart Fell is the area's second-highest hill. The route ascends on a relatively constant gradient, before descending on a rollercoaster of grassy paths to the Devil's Beef Tub. From there, it's a straightforward run home on part of the Annandale Way, a 90-kilometre trail following the River Annan from source to sea.

Distance 17km   **Ascent** 904m   **Time** 3–5 hours   **Start** Annan Water Community Hall, north of Moffat
Start latitude/longitude 55.3779, -3.4613   **Start grid reference** NT 075103   **Difficulty** 1/5 – Easy ground with few technical sections   **Bogs** 3/5 – Susceptible to bogginess after wet weather   **Terrain** Soft, grassy, rolling terrain
Map OS Explorer 330, Moffat & St Mary's Loch (1:25,000)

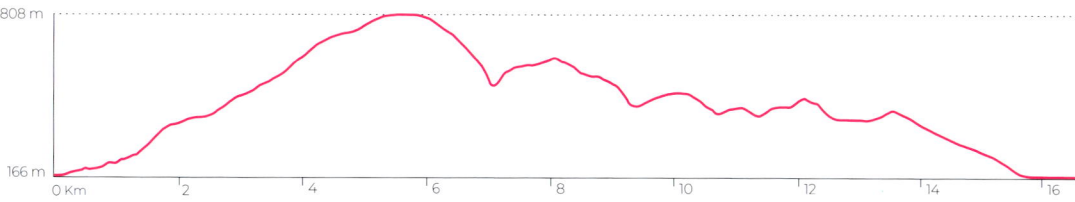

OPPOSITE *EARLY STAGES OF THE RUN* © ANDY MILTON

RUNNING TOWARDS HART FELL © ANDY MILTON

ANNANDALE WAY

HEADING UP HART FELL © ANDY MILTON

DIRECTIONS

S Starting at the Annan Water Community Hall, run north along the road for a short distance until you reach a signpost for *Hartfell Spa*. Don't get too excited: there is no sauna or jacuzzi. The spring was found in 1748 and its waters are said to have healing powers; it is worth a visit of its own. Turn right at the signpost, cross the field and follow the river uphill. These fields are usually thick with sheep. Go through a series of kissing gates, following a high deer fence.

2 Pass a bank of trees before another gate, after which you turn left up a moderately steep, grassy slope. Follow a clear trod which breaks off to the right, heading uphill. The steady, fairly runnable gradient continues up Well Rig, Bill's Cleuch and Arthur's Seat, who sound quite the trio! Ignore any other paths going off to the side and just keep heading uphill. After over 600m of climbing from the start of the route, the gradient eases. You will come across a fence running perpendicular to you; turn left to follow this fence to reach the summit of Hart Fell.

3 If it's a clear day, head east from the summit to look down into Black Hope's rugged basin, which is an excellent view. If you look at a map, you will notice the names are not like many other Scottish areas: Nubbery Knowes, Whirly Gill and Cold Grain have a very Cumbrian ring to them – a nod to the area's contested past. Follow the fence north-west from the summit until you reach a bend in the fence, where you turn left and descend. This is a brilliant, grassy descent – perfect for running. Keep the fence on your right, ignoring any gates or other openings.

4 As you descend into a steep clough, you will be running between two fences. To your left is an area protected by the Borders Forest Trust to keep deer out as a new forest regenerates. Climb steeply out of the clough which, after 70m of climbing, levels out again to give an easy run across the top of Whitehope Knowe.

ABOVE *GRASSY TRACK* © ANDY MILTON   **BELOW** *HARTFELL SPA SIGNPOST* © ANDY MILTON

❺ After 400m, the path forks: left goes through a leaning gate to the true summit of Whitehope Heights; right is your descent route. Tap the top if you fancy it and return to the path as you start another glorious (if boggy) descent into Spout Craig, sticking to the fence line on your right.

❻ You will come across a large cairn in the saddle, marking the point at which you join the Annandale Way. From here, small waymarkers will keep you on track. To continue on the full route, head west across some boggy ground and up a gradual climb to Chalk Rig Edge. The running is quick here, with very little climbing, all the way to Annanhead Hill, where a bench sits proudly above a fantastic vista of the Devil's Beef Tub and the whole area.

POINTS OF INTEREST
- **Corbett** Hart Fell, 808m
- **Donald** Whitehope Heights, 637m
- **Summit** Chalk Rig Edge, 500m
- **Summit** Annanhead Hill, 478m
- Devil's Beef Tub
- Annandale Way

HIGHLIGHTS
- Lovely runnable terrain
- Run part of the Annandale Way
- View over the Devil's Beef Tub
- Great views from Hart Fell over the Borders

GETTING THERE
Moffat is accessible by bus from Edinburgh and Glasgow. Alternatively, the nearest railway station is Lockerbie; catch a coach to go on to Moffat. Once in Moffat, there's a run of a few kilometres to the start along the Annandale Way.

Alternatively, if arriving by car, the start of the run is at is the green building marked as the Annan Water Community Hall, where there are half a dozen spaces to park.

TOP TIP
If you find yourself stuck in clag, stick to the fences and, ultimately, the Annandale Way, to aid your way around.

OTHER OPTIONS
To shorten the route, follow the directions until point **6**. At the large cairn, turn left to follow the Annandale Way downhill on a grassy trod. Cross into a field, following the waymarkers. Pass by a very cute gate and a small hut, and soon arrive at Ericstane Farm. Follow the road back to the start (14km; 746m ascent).

Another option is to start your run from Capplegill, which is on the A708 to the north-east of Moffat, and do a horseshoe around Black Hope, taking in Hart Fell and Saddle Yoke.

❼ The Devil's Beef Tub is said to be where the Border Reivers (known as 'Devils') hid stolen cattle, though it may also be due to the fact it looks like a tub used to store meat. Descend via the path to a gate, which leads to the road. Turn left here and follow the road for a short distance; there is a wide verge, so you don't need to step on tarmac.

❽ Turn right off the road, following an *Annandale Way* signpost. After another excellent descent, cross the road and join a farm track. Follow the dry stone wall downhill until you see a gate on your left. Go through this and run towards a farm, passing through it and soon crossing a river. Now it's just an 700m run along a quiet country road back to the start.

WHERE TO REFUEL
Moffat has a great selection of cafes and bakeries. My pick is **Cafe Ariete**, which provides classic Scottish cafe food like soup, toasties and a wide array of cakes.

LOVED THIS ROUTE?
The Borders Forest Trust works in this area to regenerate native woodland; find out more at **www.bordersforesttrust.org**

'The Pentland Skyline is a very accessible, easy-to-navigate route that takes in beautiful views of Edinburgh, the Firth of Forth and West Lothian. It's a long route of continuous uphill and downhill running on trails and grassy paths. A great route for various levels of hill-running experience.' ANDY DOUGLAS

Andy is a Scottish international runner based in Edinburgh. He is a five times British Mountain Running Champion and a two times winner of the World Mountain Running Cup Series.

21
PENTLAND SKYLINE
23km

The Pentland Skyline Race is one of the absolute staples of the Scottish hill racing calendar, lining up as one of the long classics series, alongside the likes of the Ochil 2000s, Stùc a' Chroin and the Arrochar Alps – each brutally hard and absolutely classic.

Starting in 1986, the Pentland Skyline Race is hosted by the Carnethy Hill Running Club, and has attracted over 4,000 runners over the years. Just a stone's throw away from Scotland's capital city, the Pentland Skyline Race is hugely popular with local trail and hill runners alike, with big names like Scottish international runner Andy Douglas, British champ Angela Mudge and bog-lover Jasmin Paris all cutting their teeth here.

The Pentland Skyline Race starts at Midlothian Snowsports Centre and climbs Caerketton Hill before joining the main circuit. However, when I asked a friend where to start this route, they mentioned the cafe at Flotterstone car park and that pretty much sealed the deal.

The route follows the elegant spine of the Pentlands, covering 23 kilometres with around 1,400 metres of ascent, making it quite a runnable route by Scottish hill running standards. Minus the odd dip into a clough, the terrain is mostly undulating on good trails, with one or two boggy sections on the less-frequented northern side of the hills. Purists will decry my missing out of Caerketton Hill, but you can add it as an out-and-back if you wish.

Whether you're staying in Edinburgh or just passing through after landing at Edinburgh Airport, the Pentland Skyline is not to be missed.

Distance 23km **Ascent** 1,424m **Time** 3–5 hours **Start** Flotterstone Visitor Centre **Start latitude/longitude** 55.8550, -3.2252 **Start grid reference** NT 234631 **Difficulty** 1/5 – Straightforward terrain without much technical ground **Bogs** 3/5 – Dry on the southern side of the route but can be boggy around Hare Hill and Black Hill **Terrain** Good paths and trails on the southern side but softer on the northern side of the route **Map** Harvey Ultramap, Pentland Hills (1:40,000)

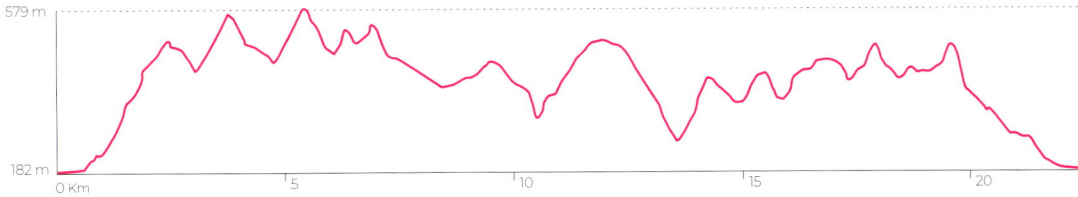

OPPOSITE *PATH ACROSS THE FLANK OF TURNHOUSE HILL* © PAUL WEBSTER

BROCKEN SPECTRE ON THE PENTLANDS RIDGE © PAUL WEBSTER

DIRECTIONS

S Start from the visitor centre (which also houses the Pentland Hills Cafe Express, whose coffees and paninis shall await your return) and head along the driveway out of the car park along the river. Turn left (following signs to *Scald Law*) and turn left again to cross a small bridge. Keep going on a sandy path among the gorse bushes and begin the long climb up Turnhouse Hill. Pass a small cluster of pines and head up the final steep stretch of foot-stepped grass. You can touch the top of Turnhouse Hill here, or you can skirt left and head straight towards the cairn.

2 Descend on a good path heading south-west into a saddle. Cross the fence and begin the climb up the bouldery peak of Carnethy Hill, which features a large cairn to shelter behind if it's windy.

3 Leave Carnethy Hill behind on a wide path into another saddle. (Here you can cut the route short by turning right and heading down into The Howe and following the track round Loganlee Reservoir below.) For those of you carrying on, cross the path and start ascending the highest peak – Scald Law.

4 Scald Law is the windcatcher of the Pentlands. It's *always* blowy up there. I remember being up here on a Carnethy 5 Hill Race and having the air sucked out of my lungs (and everywhere else, to be fair). One you've tapped the trig point, you can either continue on the main route by bearing slightly right down an eroded rocky path or do a short out-and-back to South Black Hill by bearing left down into the col. Either way, carry on over the two steep little kips – East Kip and West Kip.

5 Descend West Kip to meet a quad track known as Red Road (it is great for gravel riding). Turn right and follow this for around 1.4km before turning right off the track at a waymarker sign. Keep left at the next fork. This marks where the route starts to get a little wetter underfoot, so keep that in mind if you are heading here after a bit of rain. It isn't terrible, but you'll have some great bog marks on your legs. Ascend Hare Hill.

CARNETHY HILL FROM SCALD LAW © PAUL WEBSTER

❻ From the pudding-shaped top of Hare Hill, keep heading north-east and descend into Green Cleugh on quite a faint trod. The descent is gradual at first and steep at the end with a *proper deep bog* at the bottom. It might be best to bring a wetsuit for this bit, or just run through as fast as you can on the tufty bits. Cross the track and go straight ahead up the path in front of you, skirting the hillside and following a fence line. Ignore the first trod branching right but take the next after crossing a stile. Leave the fence behind and head through the heather. When you're almost at the summit you meet a quad track; turn right on to this then shortly afterwards turn left to reach the summit.

❼ You are now on the peated summit of Black Hill – can you guess why it is named so? Follow the north-east spur downhill on a good path, passing some grouse butts. The path starts to curve to the right; follow an old wall down to and across the river. Climb up the steep, grassy side of Bell's Hill into a recess in the contours. The path slowly bends to the right near the top of this slope towards the 406m summit.

❽ Turn sharp left at the summit and head down a fun descent into the saddle. Head up a gradual climb to Harbour Hill, following a stone wall after a gate. Once on the other side of Harbour Hill, the path bends away from the wall and meets a crossroads. Go straight across, and head up Capelaw Hill.

❾ Descend Capelaw Hill then cross a large stile and head towards a defined path and look for a green signpost for *Allermuir Hill*. Follow this to take the steep, slightly eroded path up the side of Allermuir Hill. Here you are treated to the best view of the route – an incredible vista across the reservoirs that are surrounded by all those hills you have just run over. Turn back on yourself and follow a path heading south, following a wall-cum-fence. Join the quad track and follow

it for 500m before splitting off to the right on a grassy path and joining a second quad track up Castlelaw Hill.

10 Here we are – the last top! Now, just a run back for a panini. Drop off the eastern side of Castlelaw Hill on a gravelly and awkward path downhill to rejoin the quad track. The quad track is a great descent – fast and easy underfoot. Down, down, down – all the way to a big gate at the road. Cross the road and go straight ahead through the car park then head towards a metal gate to the right of a barn. The footpath enters a lovely little woodland; continue straight ahead as you leave the trees. At the end of the next row of trees, the path splits; turn left here. Hit the road and turn left again, running downhill to rejoin the driveway where you started. Now it's just a trot back along the driveway to the car park and your warm panini.

POINTS OF INTEREST
- **Summit** Carnethy Hill, 573m
- **Summit** Scald Law, 579m
- **Summit** Allermuir Hill, 493m

HIGHLIGHTS
- Superbly runnable trails
- Excellent views over Edinburgh
- Views over the ridge from Allermuir Hill
- The paninis at the Pentland Hills Cafe Express

GETTING THERE
The easiest way to access this route is by bus; Flotterstone is on the Edinburgh to Dumfries bus route **www.travelinescotland.com**
If you're driving, be aware that Flotterstone car park can get busy, although there is an overflow car park. There is a recommended £2 donation for parking.

TOP TIP
Staying closer to Edinburgh and want a trail on the northern side of the Pentlands? Start from Balerno and take the trail to the foot of Bell's Hill.

OTHER OPTIONS
There are *loads* of paths across the Pentlands, so cutting the run short is quite straightforward. There is a road that runs through the middle of the route by the reservoirs, so if you need to cut it short, just aim for the centre road.
Alternatively, follow the main route until you reach the foot of Scald Law. Turn right and head down towards the reservoir. From there, you can pick up the route again over Black Hill. This approach works for many of the hills, as most have a track leading back to the reservoirs.

WHERE TO REFUEL
Along with **Pentland Hills Cafe Express** at the start of the route, you can also pop into the **Flotterstone Inn** itself. On the north side of the hills, **Carlyle's** (in Balerno) or **Clubbiedean's Coffee Stop** (next to Clubbiedean Reservoir) are worth a visit.

LOVED THIS ROUTE?
The Pentlands are looked after thanks to the Pentland Hills Regional Park donation scheme. Consider giving a donation at the car park **www.pentlandhills.org**

'Arran's hills are small but punchy; each peak is a perfect nubbin of rough granite. I'm constantly surprised by how rough and wild they are even after all these years of enjoying them.' LUCY WALLACE

Lucy is a Mountain Leader and wildlife guide on Arran. She's been putting down roots in this incredible landscape for 16 years but still pinches herself every day.

22
GLEN ROSA HORSESHOE, ISLE OF ARRAN *26km*

The Isle of Arran is described as 'Scotland in miniature', often named so because of its lowland–highland divide as the mountains grow more impressive as you head north.

While this is true, the description goes deeper than that. The mountains of Goatfell, Cir Mhòr, Caisteal Abhail and Beinn Tarsuinn are a fascinating mash-up of Scottish mountain landscapes. Cir Mhòr looks like the love child of the Cairngorms and the Cuillin, with sharp features and large rocky stacks that sit on its summit.

I was blown away by Arran when I first visited it. The landscape really is like nothing I have experienced, all encompassed by the sea. This means you can get some superb cloud inversions, but also some unpredictable weather.

This route largely follows the Tarsuinn Trail race route, part of the Ultra Trail Scotland event on Arran. A great bonus is that, once on Arran, you don't even need to travel to the start – the route begins in Brodick, next to the ferry port. The route follows the shoreline before heading up Arran's highest peak – Goatfell – and circling the beautiful Glen Rosa, one of Scotland's loveliest glens.

With such a varied route, you can see marine wildlife including otters and seals and, up high, you could see hen harriers or golden eagles. There is also lots of heather, which turns the hillsides a beautiful purple in August.

This route is challenging, but there are paths almost the entire way. These can be a little loose though, so care and patience is required, as well as some grippy shoes.

Distance 26km   **Ascent** 1,704m   **Time** 4–6 hours   **Start** Brodick   **Start latitude/longitude** 55.5765, -5.1393   **Start grid reference** NS 022359   **Difficulty** 4/5 – Central section between Goatfell and Cir Mhòr is steep and loose   **Bogs** 2/5 – Mostly dry but with a boggy section to finish   **Terrain** Rocky trails with a boggy descent into Glen Rosa   **Map** Harvey Superwalker, Arran (1:25,000)

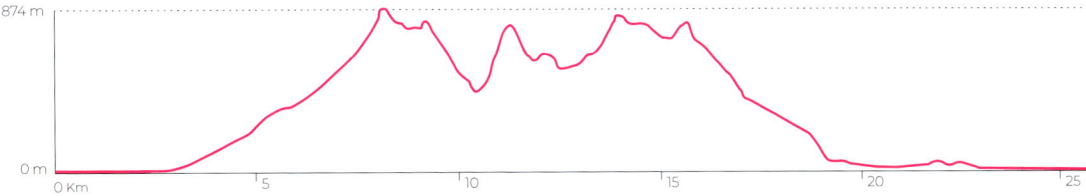

OPPOSITE *LOOKING NORTH FROM NEAR THE SUMMIT OF GOATFELL* © LEWIS TAYLOR

CAISTEAL ABHAIL AND NORTH GOATFELL © LEWIS TAYLOR

DIRECTIONS

S You might be lucky and see most of the mountains you will be heading up from the ferry terminal. Follow the shoreline along the main high street of Brodick. On your left, you will spot some of the little cafes and pubs the town has to offer. After 700m, turn right at the sign indicating the *Arran Coastal Way* or *Fisherman's Walk*. Run along the sandy trails, continuing to follow the signs for *Fisherman's Walk*. At the end of the shore, you will pop out at a car park where the Arran Mountain Rescue Team base is.

2 Cross the road and start following the signposts for *Goatfell*. The trail climbs first steadily, then more steeply, through the forest, eventually leaving the trees behind to reveal the conical peak of Goatfell. The trail is excellent all the way to the summit, all the while giving sensational views over the sea and south across the rest of the island.

3 On the summit of Goatfell the view just explodes into a cornucopia of epicness, with the amazing Cir Mhòr nestled as if in a mountainous cocoon at the centre. Cir Mhòr looks *really* intimidating from here, but it is not as bad as it looks – trust me! Continue heading north towards North Goatfell. A short distance from the top is an awkward stack of rocks; keep right to avoid the worst of it. Just beyond this, a second, much bigger, stack can be bypassed on the left.

4 Scoot up North Goatfell on a somewhat sandy trail. You now have a slightly tricky descent into the bealach. Mind your footing – some of the stones can make the trail slippery so take your time. In August, the heather in the bealach is simply gorgeous, with purple flowing down either side of it. The climb up Cir Mhòr is steep, but an obvious path zigzags its way up the side. Take the time to stop and admire the view behind you to Goatfell and, on your left, Glen Rosa.

5 The summit of Cir Mhòr is wild. You enter a natural amphitheatre of towering rock which you climb up through to reach the top. It's an incredible experience. Next, keep left at a fork in the path. (The right-hand path heads towards Caisteal Abhail, which is an obvious optional add-on.) Descend into the bealach.

ABOVE *LOOKING UP GLEN ROSA TOWARDS CIR MHÒR* **OPPOSITE** *GOATFELL SUMMIT*

❻ You will see the impressive slabs of A' Chir ahead of you. Before you reach them, branch right on to a path that will take you beneath the slabs on a bypass trail. (Do *not* try going over the slabs. There is an extremely steep section down and then up that is not advisable without climbing experience and (possibly) ropes.) The path drops down through the heather before heading slowly up again, becoming a little soggy at times. As you climb up to the next bealach, make sure to keep right to continue heading up the boulder climb to Beinn Tarsuinn. Look out for some cool rock formations!

❼ Follow the path along the grassy ridge to reach Beinn Nuis. You drop off the summit quite quickly to a flat point, where the path then heads left off the hillside and down towards the river. The path pops in and out between the boulders here, eventually flattening out and becoming a bit wet as it heads for the river.

❽ This is where it gets boggy. Keep on the right-hand side of the Garbh Allt initially. The path vanishes for a 100m section, but you then cross the river to find it again on the other side. Descend on the path, popping out at the bottom where the Garbh Allt meets the Glenrosa Water. You are now in the stunning Glen Rosa. If you look left, you will see the impressive Cir Mhòr at the end. The nicest way back is on the opposite side of the Glenrosa Water. Cross the bridge and follow the excellent trail along the river (maybe even taking a cheeky dip if it's warm).

❾ As you come to the trees, head straight on through the woods and through a wall to follow the fields. Emerge on a fire road and take a left to descend alongside the river. Shortly, you will come to a road; turn left, following signposts towards *Brodick Castle*. Retrace your steps back to Brodick.

POINTS OF INTEREST
- **Corbett** Goatfell, 874m
- **Corbett** Cir Mhòr (Great Cone), 799m
- **Corbett** Beinn Tarsuinn (Transverse Hill), 826m
- **Summit** Beinn Nuis, 792m

HIGHLIGHTS
- Unique rock formations
- Chance to explore a Scottish islands
- Great sense of adventure
- Views across the sea

GETTING THERE
Getting to Arran is an adventure in itself. The ferry runs from Ardrossan to Brodick. It is significantly cheaper to travel as a foot passenger than to take a car on to Arran; booking is pretty much essential. Ardrossan is accessible by rail or road; long-stay parking is available at Ardrossan Harbour
www.calmac.co.uk

TOP TIP
Book your ferry ticket well in advance if you are travelling by car, especially if you plan to travel at the weekend. However, going on foot can be a very rewarding experience, and doesn't require booking too far ahead.

OTHER OPTIONS
Goatfell from Brodick makes a nice out-and-back route (16km; 872m ascent). For a circular alternative: start by ascending to Goatfell as described. From the summit, head north to North Goatfell. Just beyond, turn right on to a trail through Coire Lan. Drop down to the river and come to the road. Turn right and follow the road for a short distance then turn right again on to the Arran Coastal Way and head back towards Brodick Castle and then on to Brodick (22km; 1,073m ascent).

Alternatively, from the bealach east of Cir Mhòr take the path heading south into Glen Rosa then rejoin the main route back to Brodick (21km; 952m ascent). In addition, there is another route into Glen Rosa over Beinn a' Chliabhain, which can be accessed by bearing left (south-east) in the bealach north of Beinn Tarsuinn (24km; 1,554m ascent).

If you fancy a bigger challenge, take a look at the Arran Skyline route from Ultra Trail Scotland – it is 45 kilometres in length with around 3,500 metres of ascent
www.ultratrailscotland.com

WHERE TO REFUEL
Brodick has some nice cafes and bakeries. **Wooleys of Arran** has a mighty cake selection and does a very tasty falafel wrap. Along the road, **Little Rock** serves good coffee and has a nice selection of curry pots, as well as your usual baked potatoes and sandwiches.

LOVED THIS ROUTE?
Goatfell is cared for by the National Trust for Scotland; find out how you can help support their work for wild places at www.nts.org.uk

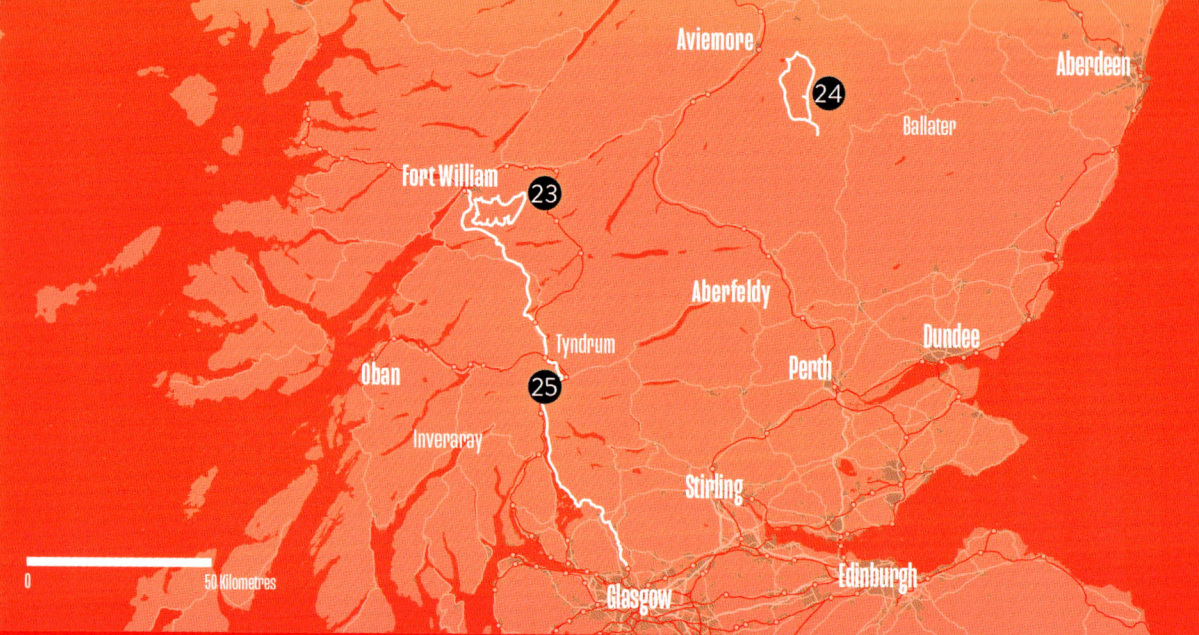

For such a small country, Scotland is full of opportunities for those who want to head out on a longer adventure in its wild places.

For those whose creativity extends beyond marked trails, the possibilities for long-distance adventures are endless, thanks to Scotland's incredible access rights, and further facilitated by the bothy network which is so cherished in this country.

Such imagination – or perhaps madness – is a long-standing feature in Scottish hill running, with innumerable challenges to test the capable runner. The Scottish Hill Runners website now lists a whopping 39 long-distance challenges including Ramsay's Round, Cairngorm 4000s, Mullardoch Round, Assynt Traverse and the Munro Round.

In addition, Scotland's Great Trails snake their way up and across the country, with notable names such as the Great Trossachs Path, the John Muir Way and the Speyside Way. They are all unique and incredible adventures.

Some of these routes will connect you to Scotland's culture, others to its wildness and nature. It is hard to find somewhere so compact with so many options.

Tranter's Round is the one that started it all in Scottish ultra-distance rounds. The inspiration for the coveted Ramsay's Round, the Tranter links some of the area's finest ridges: the Mamores, Grey Corries, the Aonachs and Ben Nevis.

Five bothies in the Cairngorms is a route I devised, and I encourage you to do the same. I adore the Cairngorms, with their raw beauty and Scandinavian vibes. I also love Scotland's bothy culture, and I found myself gazing at a map of the Cairngorm bothies and seeing a way to connect them.

The West Highland Way is a bucket-list route for many, and provides a phenomenal journey through Scotland's west coast, connecting the Central Belt to the wilds of Lochaber, all on superb trails.

There's something here for whatever adventure you want to have.

OPPOSITE *BOTHY ON LOCH LOMOND* (ROUTE 25)

MULTI-DAY ROUTES

'Tranter's Round is Scottish hill running at its finest for me. As you thread your way along the Mamores by high, technical ridges you glimpse across Glen Nevis to the Grey Corries, the Aonachs and Ben Nevis itself – all linked by equally excellent high ridges. Such an aesthetic circuit is guaranteed to sit up there with your top running memories.'   FINLAY WILD

Finlay is a hill runner and GP living in Fort William. He holds records for Tranter's Round (an excruciating 9 hours and 5 seconds) and Ramsay's Round (14 hours, 42 minutes and 40 seconds) – both of which he completed solo and unsupported.

23 TRANTER'S ROUND *63km*

In 1977, an idea was born over a pub meal. One of the people there – Chris Brasher – had just failed to complete a Bob Graham Round, his first attempt of three. Another, Charlie Ramsay, had just stolen Chris' limelight, having been invited at the last minute to support Chris' attempt, only to go on and finish the whole round in 21 hours and 52 minutes.

Chris turned to Charlie and asked whether Scotland has an equivalent to the Bob Graham Round? It did, in a way: Tranter's Round, established by Philip Tranter in 1964, was the original 24-hour walking round. Charlie had already completed the route several times in 18 hours or so. Feeling ambitious, he extended Tranter's route and thus was born Ramsay's Round – the Scottish 24-hour running round.

The Tranter, though, still holds a dear place in people's hearts and, arguably, contains the main highlights of Ramsay's Round: the incredible ridges over the Mamores, the Grey Corries and Càrn Mòr Dearg with their incredible views, and the time spent in the high mountains.

A word of warning: this route isn't for the faint-hearted. It is hard but enormously rewarding. You will need experience on technical, rough ground, quite often without a path. Do not use this description as a 100 per cent accurate guide; instead, make sure you have a map and compass and the relevant experience.

I have described the route anticlockwise and split it up into three main sections: the **Mamores**, the **Grey Corries**, and **The Aonachs and Ben Nevis**. You can do it in one go, in parts, or make it a two-day adventure, camping towards the end of the Mamores section.

Distance 63km   **Ascent** 5,933m   **Time** 1–2 days   **Start** Glen Nevis Youth Hostel   **Start latitude/longitude** 56.8000, -5.0673   **Start grid reference** NN 128718   **Difficulty** 5/5 – Significant time spent off-path; several ridges and steep climbs   **Bogs** 4/5 – Not so bad on the main ridgelines, but be prepared in the bealachs   **Terrain** A bit of everything: rough ground; grassy; rocky   **Map** Harvey 24-hour Challenge series, Charlie Ramsay Round (1:40,000)

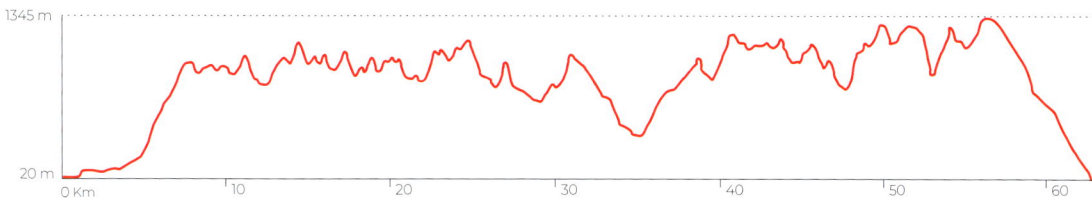

OPPOSITE *THE GREY CORRIES* © ANDY CAMPBELL

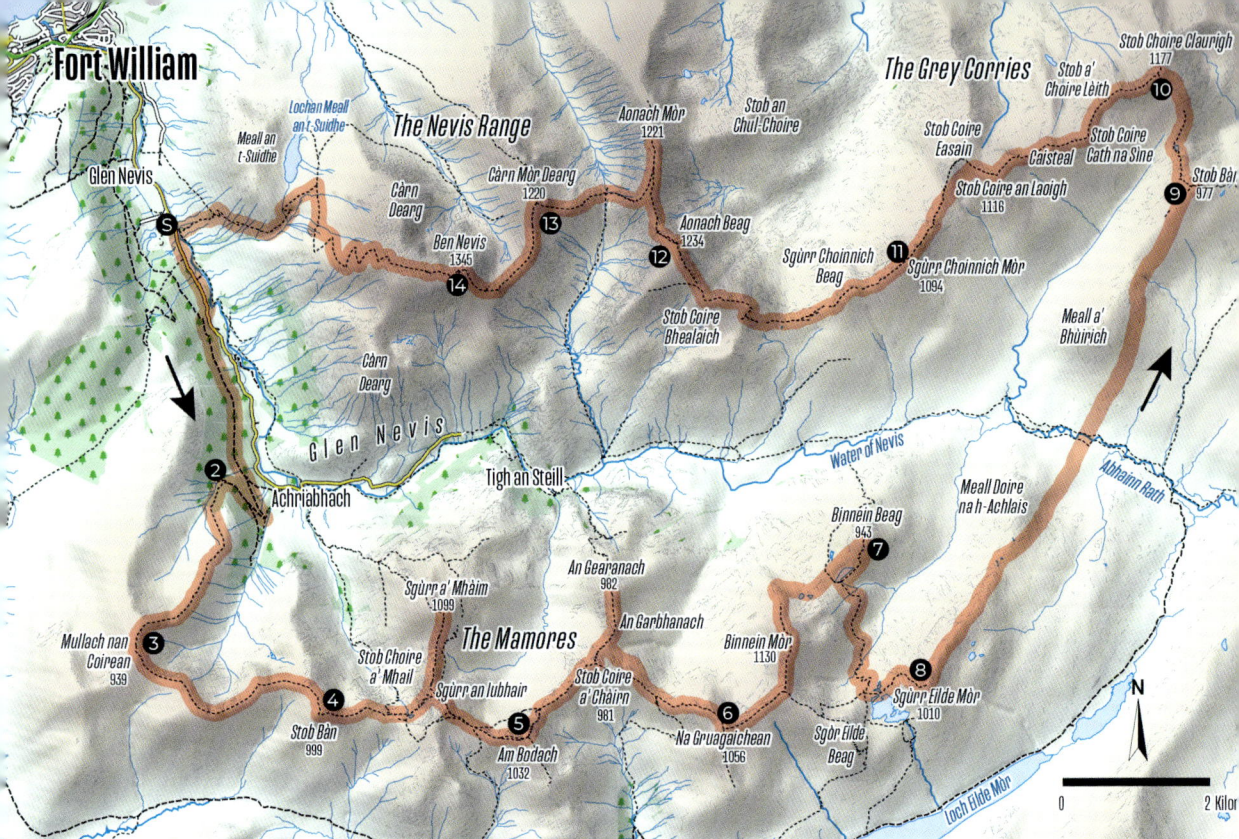

DIRECTIONS
MAMORES

S Take a quick obligatory selfie before setting off on your epic adventure. Head off up the road into the glen. After 1.2km, turn right into the forest to join a wide track (there isn't a path through the forest here, but the track is only around 60m from the road at this point). Keep right at the fork and follow the switchback.

2 Around 600m after the switchback, turn left on to a flagstone path which is marked by cairns. Be aware that there is ongoing forestry work in this area, so the paths may change over time. Cross a deer fence on to the hillside and follow the fence over boggy ground until you cross another fence. The path is now clearer, following the fence for a while before going up a steeper section to the summit of Mullach nan Coirean.

3 Follow the ridge eastwards for 3km, through initially smooth grass then rockier terrain, to reach the quartz-tipped summit of Stob Bàn.

4 Descend by a path just a few metres south of the summit and continue on down the ridge. Clip the lochan in the bealach and follow the path round to the left (be careful: it is really easy to overshoot this turn). Ascend the zigzag path then turn left at the junction to do the out-and-back to Sgùrr a' Mhàim along the Devil's Ridge. Retrace your steps to the junction and head up the subsidiary top of Sgùrr an Iubhair. Bear south-east and then follow the easy ridge to Am Bodach.

5 Head north-east down the rocky face of Am Bodach to reach Stob Coire a' Chàirn. You now have a challenging out-and-back to An Gearanach, which involves a tricky, steep section and a fairly exposed ridge. On your way back, drop into the steep bealach (between An Garbhanach and Stob Coire a' Chàirn) and then turn left, traversing first east and then south-east below Stob Coire a' Chàirn to join another bealach (between Stob Coire a' Chàirn and Na Gruagaichean). Trot along up the ridge, aiming

ABOVE *SGÙRR CHOINNICH MÒR*   **BELOW** *BINNEIN BEAG*

for the striking upper ridge of Na Gruagaichean and ignoring the paths forking left and right.

❻ Head north-east from the summit of Na Gruagaichean to reach a subsidiary 1,062m top before striking north to Binnein Mòr. The traditional route heads north-west off the summit for 300m before diving down into the corrie to reach two small lochans. This is a steep and sketchy line so, if you are just out for fun, it is better to continue further down the north-west ridge before bending to the right at around 800m elevation and heading towards the two small lochans (this option is shown on the map and GPX file). Head north-east past a larger lochan and then up the conical peak of Binnein Beag.

❼ From here, the view to the north over (the other) Stob Bàn and the Grey Corries is exquisite, so it can be a great place to set up camp so you can wake up to this view in the morning. Descend south off Binnein Beag and turn left at the

GREY CORRIES RIDGE © ANDY CAMPBELL

lochan, dropping into a beautiful corrie with ample water. Head up to some more lochans, ignoring the first left and taking the second up to Sgùrr Eilde Mòr – the last of the Mamores.

❽ There's really no nice way to get to Stob Bàn. Continue north-east from the summit of Sgùrr Eilde Mòr along the ridge, dropping to a few small pools before skirting the eastern side of Meall Doire na h-Achlais. Wade across the infamous Abhainn Rath, before traversing the eastern flank of Meall a' Bhùirich then head over damp ground up on to the ridge to reach Stob Bàn.

GREY CORRIES

❾ If you stopped to sleep at Binnein Beag, you'll probably want another after all that! Luckily, you are now rewarded for your effort by the incredible Grey Corries. From the rocky top of Stob Bàn, drop down north over steep quartz on a faint path to a couple of small lochans.

At this point you will realise what you have signed yourself up for: there is a long climb up the southern flank of Stob Choire Claurigh, with a smorgasbord of terrain from grass to scree and a fleeting path. This is a prime spot. I remember a perfect day on the Grey Corries and seeing an absolute playground of mountainous goodness stretching out before me. This summit marks the first in the Lochaber Traverse, which eventually tops out at Ben Nevis.

❿ The next section is perhaps my favourite of the route. Head west now on thrilling, undulating terrain, coming to a slabby arête just before the summit of Stob Coire an Laoigh. Go a short distance north-west towards Stob Coire Easain before dropping down to the epic granite slabs below Sgùrr Choinnich Mòr. It's a straightforward run up this, the fourteenth summit of the round.

⓫ From the summit of Sgùrr Choinnich Mòr enjoy the (mercifully) grassy descent into the bealach.

When I attempted a Lochaber Traverse a couple years ago, I tried out the trod around the base of Sgùrr Choinnich Beag and can attest it is not worth doing – just go over the hill. You are now at the crux of the round: the steep ascent up the back of Aonach Beag. You have a few options here: Spinks' Ridge (named after Nicky Spinks), Charlie's Gully, or a couple of easier but longer routes. Spinks' Ridge follows the ridgeline up terraces of rock, eventually turning into a narrow arête before becoming easier, though it is slightly eroded. Charlie's Gully can still hold snow throughout summer, so isn't ideal before July at the earliest. I have done Spinks' Ridge and found it fine (though very steep), but many may find the exposure difficult. There are a couple of gullies closer to Sgùrr a' Bhuic (a minor top) which can be easier, but require some traversing to get to. The GPX file shows the approximate line of Charlie's Gully, but common sense should be relied on more than a GPX line at this point. Once over the crux, head uphill to Stob Coire Bhealaich, before heading west then north-west to clamber up Aonach Beag. On the way, you get a sensational view towards the final summit, Ben Nevis!

THE AONACHS AND BEN NEVIS

12 From Aonach Beag, there is a great path down into the bealach and uphill to Aonach Mòr. Go back downhill from the summit of Aonach Mòr and keep right of your original ascent path. At 1,100m in height – just before the bottom of the descent – bear right towards a cairn that marks your descent into a steep-sided bealach. There's a good water source down here before the second to last climb of your round. A trod lies next to a stone wall, which takes you up a meandering route up the ridge. It steepens in places and does thin near the top, but eventually you pop out on Càrn Mòr Dearg.

13 The Càrn Mòr Dearg arête gets a lot of hype for being 'sketchy'. My father still shudders when he hears its name but, while it is a little exposed, it isn't overly difficult. There are also bypasses on the left of the technical sections. From the summit of Càrn Mòr Dearg, follow the arête to the south; the arête then curves round to the west before joining the 'back side' of the UK's highest peak. The climb up the Ben is slow, with large boulders that act like a giant staircase that has been left to fall over. Given that much of your route will have very likely been quiet, you may have to readjust a bit as you emerge on the extremely popular summit plateau, with people dressed as boilers and groups of Three Peaks baggers.

14 From the summit cairn on Ben Nevis, follow the obvious path going west that lies about 30m from the edge of the cliffs. The North Face of Ben Nevis often has snow late in the year, with large cornices suspended by nothing but the frozen snow. Stepping on them would definitely be a bad move. Begin the descent on hard, crumbled rock going west, following the line of cairns. This might be the hardest part of the whole route! You will join the Pony Track that zigzags downhill. You may be tempted to take the 'racing line'. I'm not going to stop you, but do be aware of the erosion this causes. There is another shortcut down the 'grassy bank' that's actually banned in the Ben Nevis Race, and a third which cuts the corner after the Red Burn. Be aware of your impact and remember that – while your action may not cause much damage – 100 people doing the same will. Keep left at the lochan, and follow the path downhill. Turn left to follow a signpost for the *Glen Nevis Youth Hostel* – this is 'Heart Attack Hill'. Go over the bridge, slap the hostel sign and give yourself a pat on the back – you just did Tranter's Round!

POINTS OF INTEREST
- **Munro** Mullach nan Coirean (Summit of the Corries), 939m
- **Munro** Stob Bàn (White Peak), 999m
- **Munro** Sgùrr a' Mhàim (Peak of the Rounded Hill), 1,099m
- **Munro** Am Bodach (The Old Man), 1,032m
- **Munro** Stob Coire a' Chàirn (Peak of the Corrie of the Cairn), 981m
- **Munro** An Gearanach (The Complainer), 982m
- **Munro** Na Gruagaichean (The Maidens), 1,056m
- **Munro** Binnein Mòr (Big Peak), 1,130m
- **Munro** Binnein Beag (Little Peak), 943m
- **Munro** Sgùrr Eilde Mòr (Big Peak of the Hind), 1,010m
- **Munro** Stob Bàn (White Peak), 977m
- **Munro** Stob Choire Claurigh (Peak of the Brawling Corrie), 1,177m
- **Munro** Stob Coire an Laoigh (Peak of the Calf Corrie), 1,116m
- **Munro** Sgùrr Choinnich Mòr (Big Peak of the Moss), 1,094m
- **Munro** Aonach Beag (Little Ridged Mountain), 1,234m
- **Munro** Aonach Mòr (Big Ridged Mountain), 1,221m
- **Munro** Càrn Mòr Dearg (Big Red Cairn), 1,220m
- **Munro** Ben Nevis (Venomous Mountain), 1,345m

HIGHLIGHTS
- Running an iconic Scottish hill running round
- Incredible alpine-like ridges
- Huge sense of adventure
- Stunning views everywhere
- Sitting down at the end

GETTING THERE
There is a railway station in Fort William; buses run several times a day (from May until October) from Fort William to Glen Nevis Youth Hostel **www.shielbuses.co.uk**

Alternatively, if you arrive by car, there is a pay-and-display car park at the Ben Nevis Visitor Centre which is a short distance from the youth hostel.

SPINKS' RIDGE

TOP TIP
Often the best time to run Tranter's Round or Ramsay's Round is late summer or early autumn. Snow can linger in some of the gullies for a long time, making spring escapades tricky.

OTHER OPTIONS
The obvious extension is Ramsay's Round (95km; 8,215m ascent), which takes in five extra Munros in the east around Loch Treig. The recommended Harvey map shows you the route.

To shorten the route, you have a number of options. You can complete the Mamores Round (37km; 3,117m ascent). Start from the Lower Falls car park in Glen Nevis and follow Tranter's Round route until you reach Binnein Mòr. When you reach Binnein Mòr, go back on yourself and drop east to Sgùrr Eilde Mòr. Return to the bealach and go north to Binnein Beag before bearing north-west down into the glen and running back to your starting point.

On the northern side of Tranter's Round, the Lochaber Traverse (30km; 2,735m ascent) starts just south of Corriechoille, which is accessed via a minor road south of Spean Bridge. There's a 'Wee Minister' (a small wooden statue of a minister) in the woods which marks the start (grid reference: NN 257787). It then heads up Stob Choire Claurigh, along the Grey Corries, over the Aonachs and down the Ben.

WHERE TO REFUEL
Luckily for you, the **Ben Nevis Inn** is just a short walk from the start and finish of Tranter's Round. Though, maybe ask someone to give you a piggy-back! Refuel with a Ben Nevis burger or any other pub classics. In town, the **Black Isle Bar** serves excellent pizza for hungry runners.

LOVED THIS ROUTE?
From Aonach Beag and over Ben Nevis, the land is cared for by the John Muir Trust. Learn more about their work and donate at **www.johnmuirtrust.org**

'The Cairngorms aren't about the summit cairns, they're about the space: the remoteness of the plateau, the corries, the surviving and reviving forests. This route takes a tour through the heart of the Cairngorms yet, for those with the eyes to see, opens up a lifetime of wonders still to explore.'   NEIL REID

Neil has been wandering in the Cairngorms for over 50 years and helps look after Corrour Bothy and other bothies in the area. He is a writer and a trustee of the Mountain Bothies Association.

24
FIVE BOTHIES IN THE CAIRNGORMS *64km*

Bothies are one of Scotland's most indelible features. Often situated in remote and inaccessible places, these small, usually stone-built, dwellings would once have acted as shielings for local farmers in the summertime, or as part of communities long gone. Nowadays, they provide free shelter to those on longer explorations of Scotland's wild places and should be treated with respect.

The Cairngorms are unique in that there are a large number of bothies within close proximity of each other. This route takes in five of those bothies on a breathtakingly beautiful trip through this incredible mountain range. A sixth shelter, Garbh Choire Refuge, is also close to the trail as the crow flies, but does require a hefty slog off-path to reach it.

The Lairig Ghru and Lairig an Laoigh encompass the main Cairngorm Plateau, allowing you the chance to gaze up at the giant granite mountains as you circumnavigate the range. If you are feeling super keen, you could even tag some of them on.

The route has two obvious starting points (with road access): the Linn of Dee (at the southern end of the route, near Braemar) and Glenmore (at the northern end of the route, near Aviemore). I describe the route starting from the Linn of Dee, going clockwise. Various accommodation options are available to make this a two-day adventure. Most obviously there are the bothies mentioned in the text. Be aware that some of them are only used as emergency shelters. Also, the more accessible bothies may be full; taking a lightweight tent can be a wise precaution. The youth hostel and campsite at Glenmore can be a handy overnight option if you started at the Linn of Dee.

Starting at the Linn of Dee and going clockwise, the western section of the route to Glenmore is 29 kilometres with 694 metres of ascent. From Glenmore, the eastern section of the route to the Linn of Dee is 35 kilometres with 782 metres of ascent.

Distance 64km   **Ascent** 1,476m   **Time** 2 days   **Start** Linn of Dee   **Start latitude/longitude** 56.9889, -3.5436   **Start grid reference** NO 063897   **Difficulty** 2/5 – Majority on straightforward trails bar the section at the Pools of Dee and the Chalamain Gap, which is bouldery and requires care   **Bogs** 1/5 – Almost bog-free   **Terrain** Almost entirely paths and trails   **Map** Harvey British Mountain Map, Cairngorms & Lochnagar (1:40,000).

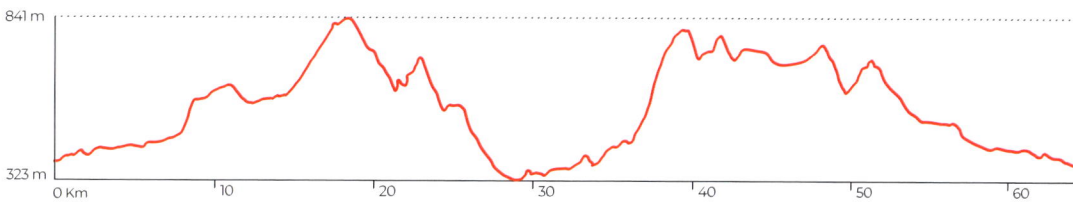

OPPOSITE *HEADING FOR CORROUR BOTHY*

GLEN DERRY WOODLAND

DIRECTIONS

S Head through the Linn of Dee car park and continue north to join the trail through the pines. This area is an ideal habitat for the incredibly rare capercaillie, a stunning bird indigenous to Scotland. Follow the trail along some boardwalks and through the trees until you reach a large vehicle track. Turn left to follow it into the panoramic Glen Lui, which gives you a first look at the splendour of the Cairngorm Plateau.

2 Cross the bridge and keep left to continue up into the glen, admiring the old Scots pines dotted by the river. With the work of the National Trust for Scotland, we will hopefully see new trees regenerating in years to come. After 5km, you will spot your first bothy – the Bob Scott Memorial Hut – on your left by the river, followed soon by Derry Lodge, an old hunting lodge. The bothy is named after Mar Lodge Estate's long-time deer stalker, who lived in a white cottage across the river.

3 Pass Derry Lodge, go over a small bridge and immediately turn left. This is the only boggy section of the route. Once through it, the track evens out into an easy gravel track, slowly gaining height as you reach the base of Carn a' Mhaim. As you round the corner of Carn a' Mhaim, the Lairig Ghru suddenly opens up ahead of you. This is probably one of the most breathtaking views at this altitude in Scotland: the dramatic Devil's Point strikes upwards to the left, while the tiny figure of Corrour Bothy sits among this giant huddle of mountains.

4 Descend gradually, after which you have the option to cross the river to see Corrour Bothy itself. Continue heading north on a narrow and winding trail that skirts the base of Ben Macdui, with excellent views to Cairn Toul on your left and Braeriach ahead. Braeriach is home to Scotland's historically longest surviving snow patch, the Sphinx, which lies at the foot of the dramatic Garbh Choire Mòr. This is also the location of Garbh Choire Refuge, but it is a long trudge from the path. The going gets increasingly tricky, with large boulders appearing as you climb.

5 After a while, the path levels out on a big boulder field, through which you will find a small set of pools known as the Pools of Dee. The 140km-

OPPOSITE *DISTANT VIEW OF HUTCHISON MEMORIAL HUT* ABOVE *RYVOAN BOTHY*

long River Dee springs from up above on Braeriach and rests here before descending to Aberdeen. Descend carefully on the boulders, noticing as the valley around you slowly narrows to a tight gap.

❻ At 600m above sea level, 21km into the route, bear right up a small path. This widens and takes you into the incredible Chalamain Gap. This dramatic gorge is full of enormous boulders. It's incredibly impressive, but can be dangerous in winter conditions when the avalanche risk is high. Pass through the gap and follow a superb trail downhill, alongside the river. At the time of writing, the next section has been under repair due to a landslip, but is still navigable. Cross the road and continue to descend on magical trails down to Glenmore.

❼ From Glenmore, follow the forestry tracks east into the Ryvoan Pass. The pinewoods slowly thin to reveal a beautiful woodland and incredible views south to the Cairngorms themselves. Descend into the pass and enjoy the mysterious An Lochan Uaine – the Green Lochain. Bear left here, following the wide track as it slowly climbs. You will reach a fork with a signpost pointing to the right for *Lairig an Laoigh*; continue straight ahead here to see Ryvoan Bothy.

❽ From Ryvoan Bothy, return to the junction and turn left, following the signpost for *Lairig an Laoigh*. This track is fairly flat for 3km but later begins to climb up the slope of Bynack More.

❾ As the path flattens out you will reach a path junction; you can see Bynack More ahead from here. You can turn right here to include an easy 5km out-and-back to the summit of Bynack More; otherwise, keep left to drop into the glen. Follow the Allt Dearg south to the Fords of Avon Refuge. The refuge's modern look is thanks to a renovation by the Mountain Bothies Association in 2011. It is a tight fit – very much an emergency shelter rather than a bothy – and has saved a number of lives over the years.

❿ Cross the River Avon to follow the path as it gently rises alongside the Allt an t-Seallaidh. Eventually, you will reach a col where the Lairig an Laoigh gives way to Glen Derry. Descend on a good path and, 1.5km later, you will reach a path junction. Turn right here, going into a corrie. This is where you'll find the final bothy of the trip, the Hutchison Memorial Hut, in the spectacular Coire Etchachan.

⓫ Retrace your steps from the bothy to the path junction and turn right. This is a supremely runnable trail through Glen Derry, passing through a small woodland before crossing the Derry Burn to meet the outward route. Turn left to pass Derry Lodge and follow the track through Glen Lui back to the Linn of Dee.

POINTS OF INTEREST
- Bob Scott Memorial Hut
- Corrour Bothy
- Ryvoan Bothy
- Fords of Avon Refuge
- Hutchison Memorial Hut
- Glen Lui
- Lairig Ghru
- Lairig an Laoigh
- Glen Derry
- Chalamain Gap
- Ryvoan Pass
- Pools of Dee
- An Lochan Uaine

HIGHLIGHTS
- Stunning views
- Entering the Lairig Ghru
- Finding the Pools of Dee – the source of the River Dee
- Mix of accessibility and remoteness
- Visiting the bothies

GETTING THERE
The route starts at the Linn of Dee. The nearest public transport (a bus from Aberdeen) is at Braemar, which is approximately 10 kilometres to the east. Alternatively, there is a pay-and-display car park at the Linn of Dee. An alternative starting point is at the northern end of the route at Glenmore. A bus runs from Glenmore to Aviemore, where there is a railway station.

TOP TIP
If you want to stay at one of the bothies overnight, I'd recommend starting a little later on your first day and staying at the most famous – Corrour. Alternatively, you could try Ryvoan, but this is much more accessible and can easily be full. Either way, pack a small tent or bivvy bag, just in case there isn't enough space inside!

OTHER OPTIONS
There are a couple of ways to extend this route. Firstly, you can add on a loop of four Munros to the western section of the route. From point **4** head to Corrour Bothy and continue on past it to climb up the steps to the Devil's Point, which is to the left at the head of the climb. Run north along the ridge over the bouldered shoulder of Cairn Toul, taking in the sweeping views. Continue on over Sgòr an Lochain Uaine and the hulking giant of Braeriach. Descend Braeriach and rejoin the main route just before the Chalamain Gap. (This extension adds 8km and 951m of ascent to the standard route.)

Secondly, you can take in some more Munros in the eastern part of the route. From point **11** head west past the Hutchison Memorial Hut and climb to the bealach at the foot of Beinn Mheadhoin. Turn left up the path, which climbs for a short distance before levelling out, enjoying an amazing view down into Loch Etchachan. On your left, make sure you spot the small bump called Creagan a' Choire Etchachan. As you pass it, leave the path and skirt the foot of this little bump, heading up to Derry Cairngorm. The path then descends Derry Cairngorm heading south-east then south back to Derry Lodge. (This extension adds 2km and 497m of ascent to the standard route.)

WHERE TO REFUEL
There are so many options for you to refuel and rest up. If you are finishing at Glenmore, head to the **Pine Marten Bar** or the **Lochain Bar** at Glenmore Lodge for some food and drink.

If you are going to Aviemore, check out the **Old Bridge Inn** or, if buffets are what you need, **La Taverna**.

LOVED THIS ROUTE?
Much of this area is part of the UK's largest National Nature Reserve, Mar Lodge Estate, which is managed by the National Trust for Scotland. You can learn more at **www.nts.org.uk**

All of the bothies, except for the Bob Scott Memorial Hut, are cared for by the Mountain Bothies Association. You can learn more about this charity at **www.mountainbothies.org.uk**

OPPOSITE *UPPER GLEN DERRY*

'The West Highland Way is a constantly evolving trail. The gentle meander to Drymen gives way to breathtaking views off Conic Hill. As the trail goes north, I find myself at peace on the remote moors towards Glen Coe, while the Munros reach out to the sky around you. No two days on the trail are the same; I can never tire of it.' — JAMES STEWART

James is a North-Lanarkshire-based ultrarunner and coach. He has competed for Great Britain in 24-hour racing and holds records on the Fife Coastal Path and the John Muir Way.

25
WEST HIGHLAND WAY – SCOTLAND'S CLASSIC TRAIL *153km*

The West Highland Way. It is *the* trail in Scotland. It was also the first long-distance trail in Scotland (it opened in 1980).

While you might be thinking this is a rather peculiar addition to this book (too popular; not that challenging; a bit too 'runnable'), I personally feel that the West Highland Way is a brilliant adventure and a great way to see the changing Scottish landscape.

From the bustle and culture of Glasgow, which is near the start at Milngavie, around the rolling Campsie Fells, along the stunning Loch Lomond and into the Highlands, the Way really is a great adventure. Walkers usually complete the Way in about a week, but we runners can trot along and be done within three or four days. For ease, I have split the directions into four sections; each section could be run in a day. The whole trail is waymarked, so I provide a general overview of the route rather than more detailed directions. I have described the route from south to north, which is the traditional way of completing the Way. It also means the landscape gets more dramatic as you go.

Given how popular the Way is, I recommend booking any accommodation in advance. If you want to camp but don't want the hassle of carrying your gear, consider using a baggage transfer company. If you want to wild camp, be aware that some areas of the route are covered by wild camping bye-laws www.lochlomond-trossachs.org/things-to-do/camping

The West Highland Way website is a great resource for planning your adventure: www.westhighlandway.org

Distance 153km **Ascent** 3,284m **Time** 3–5 days **Start** Milngavie **Finish** Fort William **Start/finish latitude/longitude** 55.9417, -4.3184/56.8159, -5.1145 **Start/finish grid reference** NS 553745/NN 100737 **Difficulty** 2/5 – Almost entirely on excellent trails bar an awkward rooty section at Loch Lomond **Bogs** 1/5 – Almost bog-free **Terrain** Almost entirely paths and trails **Map** Vertebrate Publishing Guidemap, West Highland Way (1:40,000)

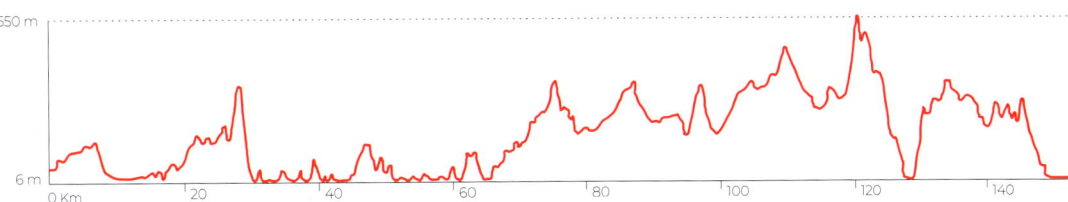

OPPOSITE *ENTERING GLEN COE*

THE BEINN DORAIN MUNROS

DIRECTIONS
MILNGAVIE TO ROWARDENNAN

S Pass under the archway in Milngavie to start your grand adventure and enter Mugdock Country Park, a lovely spot with lots of trees and popular with local trail runners. The clearly marked path heads north-west, eventually leaving the trees behind and giving a grand view of the Campsie Fells. Here, the West Highland Way and the John Muir Way, a 213-kilometre trail which runs from Helensburgh to John Muir's birthplace in Dunbar, briefly follow the same route. Just after Dumgoyne, you will pass a little honesty box at the brilliantly named deli, Turnip the Beet.

2 You switch between on-road and off-road on the way to Drymen. If you fancy a pit stop here, you do have to turn off the trail. We thought that the trail went through Drymen and were sorely disappointed (and hungry) when it did not! You are now on some large fire roads and climbing steadily, heading towards Loch Lomond. As the track levels out, you will see the steep Conic Hill ahead, which is a tough climb for such a modest peak.

3 Drop down from Conic Hill into Balmaha and make sure to stop at St Mocha for a toastie (or two). Do not underestimate the run to Rowardennan. The path along Loch Lomond rises and falls like a coastal path, with short, steep ascents and quick descents. (The section from Milngavie to Rowardennan is 43km with 797m of ascent.)

ROWARDENNAN TO TYNDRUM

4 The section from Rowardennan is a bit of a tough old slog along Loch Lomond, made up for by the gorgeous oak woodland surrounding it. Initially on some good trails, it becomes increasingly rooty and rocky, making smooth running difficult. You will pass the picturesque Doune Byre Bothy and are soon rewarded at the northern end of the loch by lovely grassy pasture, with easy access to the water to soothe sore feet!

5 Follow the river past Inverarnan, sticking to the path that runs behind the campsite. This becomes a wide 4x4 track going steadily uphill. Eventually, you pass beneath the A82, continuing to climb to a great viewpoint overlooking the road, giving great views back to Ben Lomond – a good feeling! Enter the woodland and descend towards the road. Don't be fooled – it isn't all downhill. You can imagine my disappointment – on tired legs, looking at the lovely downhill on my watch – to find yet

MEALL AN T-SUIDHE

another tiny rise in the terrain. Once across the road, it is a flat run to Tyndrum, where there will be a fine chippy waiting for you at the Real Food Cafe. (The section from Rowardennan to Tyndrum is 41km with 939m of ascent.)

TYNDRUM TO KINLOCHLEVEN

❻ I love this section. Head north from Tyndrum, going uphill. You really get the sense you are off into the Highlands: the big hills rise around you, with increasingly expanding views.

❼ Stop off at the hotel in Bridge of Orchy for a scone and a brew before following the road behind it for a short section then turning left up a steadily rising track. The view from the top of this climb over Victoria Bridge and the Munros Stob Ghabhar and Stob a' Choire Odhair is staggering. Descend a rocky path to the road, which becomes a cobbled track over Rannoch Moor into Glen Coe.

❽ Glen Coe's reputation is rightly legendary. Once at the Kingshouse Hotel, make sure you stop for a beverage and enjoy the views up the glen – they are amazing. Run parallel to the main road, eventually turning off to head up the notorious Devil's Staircase. Perhaps because I am a runner with a lighter pack, I didn't find this climb as heinous as many walkers warn. Take in the view over the Mamores before dropping down the long, constant track into Kinlochleven. (The section from Tyndrum to Kinlochleven is 45km with 977m of ascent.)

KINLOCHLEVEN TO FORT WILLIAM

❾ This section starts with a climb – follow the road out of Kinlochleven and go over the large bridge, heading north-west. Turn right up a wooded path, climbing steadily until you pop out of the trees. Hit a large track and head left, still climbing but less steeply. This track curves around the base of the Mamores, the venue for Ramsay's Round and the Ring of Steall. This section really does feel far from everywhere. The track curves round to the north then you reach a junction.

❿ Turn right up a steep little path to an excellent viewpoint over the UK's highest peak: Ben Nevis. Run along the undulating path until you hit the forest, before dropping all the way down into Glen Nevis. Turn left once you hit tarmac and run into the town, along High Street and plop your bum down on the bench next to a statue of an old guy rubbing his feet. Congratulations! Now, get yourself into the Black Isle Bar for a pizza and a well-earned pint. (The section from Kinlochleven to Fort William is 24km with 571m of ascent.)

ABOVE *BUACHAILLE ETIVE MÒR*

ABOVE *WOODLAND TRAIL* **BELOW** *CONIC HILL*   **ABOVE** *LOOKING OVER LOCH LEVEN* **BELOW RIGHT** *AT THE START*

25 WEST HIGHLAND WAY – SCOTLAND'S CLASSIC TRAIL

NEAR TYNDRUM

POINTS OF INTEREST
- **Summit** Conic Hill, 361m
- Loch Lomond
- Loch Leven
- Devil's Staircase
- Milngavie
- Drymen
- Balmaha
- Tyndrum
- Kinlochleven
- Fort William

HIGHLIGHTS
- Leaving the towns behind on Conic Hill
- The section from Tyndrum to Glen Coe
- Entering the Highlands on foot
- Devil's Staircase – both the climb and views
- Coffee and scones in Bridge of Orchy

GETTING THERE
Using public transport is a great option for this route – both Milngavie and Fort William have railway stations.

TOP TIP
Book accommodation in advance, as during high season you might find a few to be very busy.

OTHER OPTIONS
Not keen on the full route? You can split the route in half, which is what the Highland Fling Race and the Devil o' the Highlands do.

If you fancy a challenge in the early part of the route, why not take on one of Scotland's most popular Munros: Ben Lomond. Follow the route described on pages 105–109, to take the scenic route up the Ptarmigan Ridge.

To add in some extra mountains to your day, there is a great alternative route to replace a section starting to the north of Tyndrum and finishing at Bridge of Orchy. Follow the track north from Tyndrum, running next to the railway line, for 5.5km to reach a small bridge. Don't cross the bridge; instead, turn right towards the railway viaduct and follow the rocky track into the glen. Keep right as it bends around, eventually coming to a small

LEFT TRACK TO BRIDGE OF ORCHY **ABOVE** GOATS

weir. At this point, turn left and head straight up the grassy slope to Beinn Mhanach. Drop down west into a bealach and north up to Meall Buidhe, following the ridge over Beinn Achaladair and Beinn an Dothaidh. In the bealach, there is a path that descends west back to Bridge of Orchy, where you return to the West Highland Way. (This extension adds 18km and 1,538m of ascent to the standard route.)

If you get to Kinlochleven and realise that you're not quite tired enough you could try an alternative route through the Mamores. Once you arrive on the wide path above Kinlochleven, turn left, cross a bridge and, as you climb for a short section, look out for a cairn on the right. Turn right here, heading north. This path, which alternates between trail and a little bog, climbs to the summit of Sgùrr an Iubhair. Head west over Stob Bàn and Mullach nan Coirean, before dropping down into the forest and rejoining the West Highland Way in Glen Nevis. (This extension adds 1km and 856m of ascent to the standard route.)

WHERE TO REFUEL
Early in the trail, there are loads of honesty boxes, where you are trusted to leave money in exchange for snacks. It is amazing!

On the first section, I'd recommend stopping at the **St Mocha Coffee Shop and Ice Cream Parlour** for lunch and the **Clansmen Bar** at the **Rowardennan Hotel** for dinner. **Tyndrum's Real Food Cafe** is famous among walkers and will serve a feast after a long day. On the penultimate stretch, the **Bridge of Orchy Hotel** and the **Kingshouse Hotel** will serve a fantastic coffee, while **Kinlochleven's Getaway Inn** will fuel you for the final push. Once you reach Fort William, dive into the **Black Isle Bar** for a well-deserved pizza.

LOVED THIS ROUTE?
The West Highland Way is cared for by a number of public bodies, led by the Loch Lomond and the Trossachs National Park. You can support the upkeep of the trail at **www.westhighlandway.org/support**

APPENDIX

MORE LIKE THIS

Here's some more ideas for places to run in the areas covered by this book.

NORTH WEST HIGHLANDS
Torridon Trail
Torridon is a haven for stunning landscapes. This loop allows the runner to enjoy the view from many perspectives. Starting from a car park on the A896, a trail runs around the back of the multi-spired mountain of Liathach to the village of Torridon. After a pit stop, cross the road to climb to Loch an Eoin before descending back to the car park.

Stac Pollaidh
The rugged peak of Stac Pollaidh sits on the remote road to Achiltibuie. The mountain's odd shape is thanks to its summit ridge poking above an old ice sheet as the glacier rubbed its sides smooth. The route can be done as a simple loop of the base, or some may wish to take a minor scramble on to the ridge.

Ben Wyvis
Ben Wyvis is not far from Inverness and is close to the train station at Garve. It is a solitary Munro, giving it brilliant views of the surrounding area. A good path wriggles its way up the sprawling mountain before levelling out to provide an excellent run to the top.

WESTERN HIGHLANDS
Cow Hill
Along with the Half Ben Nevis and Meall an t-Suidhe races, Cow Hill makes up number three of the local Triple Hirple race series in Fort William. Excellent trails from bottom to top and all around make this a great leg stretcher from the town.

Beinn Fhada
Sitting at the end of Glen Shiel, Beinn Fhada (Long Mountain) sits above Loch Duich and can be made into a great circular trail run. Starting and finishing at Morvich, head up either via the glen or up the face and back the other way, with a couple of fun scrambles thrown in.

The Quiraing
The Quiraing is a fascinating jumble of rock from an ancient landslide on the northern side of Skye. Starting close to Flodigarry, head past Loch Langaig and keep left, heading towards the rocky outcrops. From there you can loop around The Prison, or you can go on and bear right to go higher on to the tops.

CAIRNGORMS
Cairngorm 4000s
This classic ski route has become a gem in the world of long-distance hill running challenges. The route takes in the plateau and the dramatic ridge between Cairn Toul and Breariach. You can start in the ski centre car park and take in Cairn Gorm, Ben Macdui, Cairn Toul, Sgòr an Lochain Uaine and Braeriach. It is *epic*.

Craigellachie
Craigellachie National Nature Reserve is on the edge of Aviemore, just up from the youth hostel. It makes an ace little run from town, with sensational views for its diminutive size. The first part goes up through a beautiful woodland before breaking on to a clear summit with an amazing vista of the Cairngorms.

Glen Shee
Glen Shee is a great place to experience the Scottish mountains without having to do too much ascent to get there. The road tops out at over 600 metres, so getting to the tops isn't so hard. There are great runs over The Cairnwell and Carn Aosda in the west, or Glas Maol and its neighbours in the east.

OPPOSITE *NEAR THE TOP OF SGÙRR AN LOCHAIN* (ROUTE 08)
PREVIOUS PAGE *DISTANT BEINN A' GHLO FROM BLAIR ATHOLL* (ROUTE 13) © PAUL WEBSTER

PATH ALONG LOCH LOMOND (ROUTE 25)

SOUTHERN HIGHLANDS
Bridge of Orchy 5
This is an understated challenge but it's slowly becoming a favourite of many Scottish hill runners. Start the route from the Bridge of Orchy Hotel and take on this superb route up Beinn Dòrain, over to Beinn Mhanach and on to the Achaladair Munros, bobbing along the ridge to Beinn an Dothaidh.

Glen Lyon Horseshoe
On the south side of Glen Lyon lies the impressive Ben Lawers range, but to the north is the excellently runnable Glen Lyon Horseshoe, touching the top of four Munros. Starting in Invervar, the route can be done clockwise or anticlockwise over Càrn Gorm, Meall Garbh, Càrn Mairg and Meall na Aighean.

Ben Vorlich
Ben Vorlich and its neighbour Stùc a' Chroin are a favourite of those in the Stirlingshire area. Heading up from Loch Earn, you can make a loop of Ben Vorlich up a great track and around it on a grassy path. To extend the route, a short scramble up to Stùc a' Chroin is worth the extra effort.

CENTRAL AND SOUTHERN SCOTLAND
Dumyat
Dumyat is an iconic hill at the very edge of the Ochil Hills. Standing proudly above the University of Stirling, it is a favourite of local hill runners, giving excellent views over the Wallace Monument, Stirling and the Forth Valley. There are many ways up – from the university, through the woods and back via the 'grassy ridge' is a firm favourite of mine.

Lomond Hills
There are so many options in the Lomond Hills, which sit in Fife on the east coast. You could start at Falkland Palace and goes up the main track to West Lomond. You can then drop off to the north and follow a trail along a wall into the woods back to the palace. The hills are also home to the hotly contested Devil's Burdens Relay in January.

Gypsy Glen
The Borders are a paradise for mountain bikers, whose mecca at Glentress also makes for some top-class trail running. Out of Peebles, though, there is a route south up to Birkscairn Hill which then drops down to Cardrona before following a cycle lane back to Peebles.

MULTI-DAY ROUTES
Skye Trail
Wiggling from the top to the toe of Skye, the Skye Trail is a superb route which takes in some of the most dramatic features of the island. You will pass the Quiraing, follow the Trotternish Ridge, go through the Cuillin and run around a section of coast on this superb three-to-four-day adventure.

Mullardoch Round
If it's a long day in wild country you're after, you cannot get much better than the Mullardoch Round – a whopping challenge in one of Scotland's wildest places. Circumnavigating Loch Mullardoch, the route takes in 12 Munros on technical ground. It can be split into two days, or – if you're Finlay Wild – 7 hours and 40 minutes!

SPIDEAN CÒINICH (ROUTE 02)

AN LOCHAN UAINE (ROUTES 11 AND 24)

CONTACTS
The following is a list of handy contacts, websites, accommodation providers, shops, guides, and other resources.

TOURIST INFORMATION
For most of the information you require, **www.visitscotland.com** is a great resource, along with the local information centres.

ACCOMMODATION
Scotland has a large network of caravan and camping sites, youth hostels and hotels.
www.hostellingscotland.org.uk
www.scottish-hostels.com
www.campingandcaravanningclub.co.uk
www.caravanclub.co.uk
www.visitscotland.com

PUBS AND RESTAURANTS
Here are some key pubs and bars in Scotland you should have on your radar.
Ben Nevis Inn
www.ben-nevis-inn.co.uk
Clachaig Inn, Glen Coe
www.clachaig.com

Old Bridge Inn, Aviemore
www.oldbridgeinn.co.uk
Pine Marten Bar, Glenmore
www.facebook.com/PineMartenBarGlenmore
Seumas' Bar, Sligachan Hotel, Isle of Skye
www.sligachan.co.uk
The Drovers Inn, Loch Lomond
www.droversinn.co.uk
The Old Mill Inn, Pitlochry
www.theoldmillpitlochry.co.uk

ACCESS AND NAVIGATION
Scotland has incredible access rights, but please act responsibly.
Scottish Outdoor Access Code
www.outdooraccess-scotland.scot
Harvey Maps
www.harveymaps.co.uk
Ordnance Survey
www.ordnancesurvey.co.uk

FOREST VIEWS (ROUTE 10)

WEATHER
Scotland has extremely changeable weather, so always be prepared with a plan B and check the forecast. Here are appropriate resources for outdoor pursuits.
www.mwis.org.uk
www.mountain-forecast.com
www.metoffice.gov.uk
www.sais.gov.uk

GUIDES
There are some specific trail- and hill-running guides available in Scotland.
Trail Running Scotland
www.trailrunningscotland.com
Girls on Hills
www.girlsonhills.com
Skye Running Tours
www.skyerunningtours.co.uk

SHOPS
There are some specific running stores in Scotland, as well as a range of general outdoor shops.
www.run4it.com
www.runandbecome.com
www.tiso.com
www.ellis-brigham.com
www.cotswoldoutdoor.com
www.alpkit.com

RUNNING WEBSITES
Scotland's rich history of hill running and long-distance challenges has produced an incredible community of runners. There are two key websites for those interested in either racing in Scotland or taking on a big challenge.
www.scottishhillrunners.uk
www.gofar.org.uk